CONSTITUTIONALISM
AND THE RULE OF LAW
IN AMERICA

The Heritage Foundation
LEADERSHIP FOR AMERICA

© 2009 by The Heritage Foundation
214 Massachusetts Avenue, NE
Washington, DC 20002-4999
202.546.4400 ● heritage.org

Printed in the United States of America

ISBN: 978-0-89195-132-2
Cover photo by James Steidl, 2006 (Photolia)

CONSTITUTIONALISM AND THE RULE OF LAW IN AMERICA

By Herman Belz

TABLE OF CONTENTS

PREFACE

*T*hroughout most of human history, the rules by which life was governed were usually determined by force and fraud: He who had the power—whether military strength or political dominance—made the rules. The command of the absolute monarch or tyrannical despot *was* the rule and had the coercive force of the law. Rulers made up false stories and rationalizations to convince their subjects to accept their rules as the will of God, which was not to be contradicted. This is still the case in many parts of the world, where the arbitrary rulings of the dictator are wrongly associated with the rule of law.

The rule of law—a principle that itself is quite old and long predates the United States—is the general concept that government as well as the governed are subject to the law and that all are to be equally protected by the law. Its roots can be found in classical antiquity. The vast difference between the rule of law and that of individual rulers and tyrants has been a central theme in the writings of political philosophers from the beginning.

In Anglo–American history, the concept was already expressed in the Magna Carta in 1215. The idea that the law is superior to human rulers is the cornerstone of English constitutional thought as it developed over the centuries. It can be found elaborated in the great 17th century authorities on British law, Henry de Bracton, Edward Coke, and William Blackstone. The ultimate outcome of the Glorious Revolution of

1688 in England was permanently to establish that the king was subject to the law.

The idea was transferred to the American colonies through numerous writers and jurists, and can be seen expressed throughout colonial pamphlets and political writings. The classic American expression of the idea comes from the pen of John Adams when he wrote the Massachusetts Constitution of 1780, in which the powers of the Commonwealth are divided in the document "to the end it may be a government of laws, not of men." It is hard to come up with a simpler definition.

The idea of a constitution was not new either and goes far back in Western political thought. The concept can be found in Greek philosophy, suggested in Aristotle's classification of "regimes" based on the rule of one (monarchy or tyranny), the few (aristocracy or oligarchy), and the many (democracy). It implied certain arrangements of the offices in the city or state. Similar ideas can be found in the works of Cicero and other Roman writers.

The key turn in constitutional history comes with the development by John Locke and others of a natural law theory including inalienable personal rights. If certain rights belong to each person by nature, then it follows that legitimate governments are organized to protect those rights. England was moving in this direction, but the full implications of this constitutional development first appeared in the principles and institutions of the American Founding.

In appealing to their constitutional rights, the American colonists were confronted with the practical problem that the British didn't really have a constitution at all—at least not a comprehensive, written constitution as we understand it. Americans wanted such a document, under the rule of law, that would create an enduring structure and process for securing their rights and liberties and spell out the divisions of powers within government and its overall limits. What's more, that constitution would be above ordinary legislation, which is to say above the ordinary, changing actions of government. That is what they meant by "constitution," and that, by definition, meant a framework of limited government.

In this monograph, Herman Belz tells the story of this development and explains the view of the rule of law and constitutionalism that was established in the United States. It is no coincidence that the rule of law and constitutionalism have always been central to our politics and political life. From the legacy of America's Founders through the challenge of our Civil War, strained under the attack of Progressive and then New Deal reformers, revived under modern conservatism and the argument for constitutional originalism, these principles remain just as relevant and controversial as they were in 1787.

But something fundamental has changed in this debate and in how we understand these principles. Belz writes that Americans "have reason to be concerned about the survival of the Constitution." We may be distinctive in our attachment to a written constitution, but that does not detract from our solemn responsibility to maintain *this* Constitution. After all, "the fidelity that Americans profess rests on the conviction that the Constitution of the Founding establishes institutions of republican self-government that are indispensable to the preservation of individual and national freedom."

It is hard to think of a scholar better qualified to defend these principles and this Constitution than Herman Belz. He is a professor of U.S. and constitutional history at the University of Maryland and Academic Director of the James Madison Memorial Fellowship Foundation. His books include *The Webster–Hayne Debate on the Nature of the Union: Selected Documents* (2000); *A Living Constitution or Fundamental Law: American Consti-*

tutionalism in Historical Perspective (1998); *Abraham Lincoln, Constitutionalism, and Equal Rights During the Civil War Era* (1998); and *Equality Transformed: A Quarter Century of Affirmative Action* (1991). He is also the co-author (with Alfred H. Kelly and Winifred A. Harbison) of the standard text in the field of American constitutional history, *The American Constitution: Its Origins and Development* (1991), now in its seventh edition.

This publication is part of a series of occasional essays and booklets published by The Heritage Foundation, under the auspices of the B. Kenneth Simon Center for American Studies, on the "First Principles" of the American tradition of ordered liberty that we seek to conserve "for ourselves and our posterity," as it says in our Constitution. Publications cover a range of themes and topics, each aimed at explaining our most primary ideas—ideas that often have been forgotten or rejected—and considering what those principles should mean for America today.

The series is motivated by a powerful observation: Those who lead our nation today—and those who will lead it tomorrow—must *know* and *understand* our first principles if they mean to vindicate those principles and see to it that they once again guide our country.

The rule of law may be the most significant and influential accomplishment of Western constitutional thinking. The meaning and structure of our Constitution embody this principle. Nowhere expressed yet evident throughout, the United States Constitution depends on this bedrock concept: the first principle on which the American legal and political system was built.

The design, forms, and institutions of that system—what is called the *constitutionalism* of the American Founders—define the necessary conditions of the rule of law and limited government, and hence liberty. That constitutionalism, made up of the various structural concepts embodied in the Constitution of the United States, comprises one of our most important first principles. The rule of law and constitutionalism are important concepts not because they are old, or unique, or exclusively ours for that matter, but because they form the architecture of freedom.

Matthew Spalding
Director, B. Kenneth Simon Center for American Studies
First Principles Series Editor

INTRODUCTION

*T*he Founding Fathers' legacy to the American people is a depository of limited constitutional government intended to secure national independence, responsible individual liberty, and social freedom. In the words of poet Robert Frost, the legacy was a "gift outright," one that was neither intended to be nor capable of being repaid. Intrinsic to the deed of gift nevertheless was a challenge to future generations of Americans to preserve the rights and liberties of a free people against the contingencies of history and the imperfections of human nature.

The Founders understood that a necessary relationship exists between liberty and authority in a rightly ordered republican constitution. In a time of rising democratic sentiment that threatened to spill over into mob rule, Abraham Lincoln underscored this fact in observing that "the strongest bulwark of any Government, and particularly of those constituted like ours," is "the *attachment* of the People."[1] To strengthen that attachment and preserve civil and religious liberty, Lincoln urged reverence for the Constitution and the laws.

In our own troubled times, a proper regard for the opinions of the Founders, and for the efforts of generations of

---

[1.] Abraham Lincoln, "Address Before the Young Men's Lyceum of Springfield, Illinois," January 27, 1838, in *Abraham Lincoln: His Speeches and Writings*, ed. Roy P. Basler (Cleveland: World Publishing Co., 1946), p. 80. Emphasis in original.

I

Americans who have responded to the challenge of the Founding, requires reflection on the meaning of the Constitution and the rule of law if the blessings of liberty are to be preserved in the 21st century. The purpose of this essay is to promote this end through intellectual inquiry into the tradition of constitutional practical reason and civic virtue on which American republican freedom depends.

The framing and ratification of the U.S. Constitution marked the establishment of fundamental law based on principles of reason and justice as embodied in institutions of liberty and consent that took root in the American colonies in the 17th and 18th centuries. Acting with audacity, foresight, and prudence, the Founders constructed a stable constitutional order that gave enduring effect to the revolutionary principles on which the American people's claim to national independence rested. Representing the rights, interests, and moral values of constituents in local communities, the Framers created a federal republican Union with authority to legislate for the common good and public interest of the country as a whole. At the same time, recognizing the practical necessity and political virtue of local self-government in republican America, the Constitution's authors confirmed, while placing reasonable limits upon, the authority of the state governments to regulate domestic and municipal affairs.

Accepting the challenge implicit in the Founders' legacy, the American people in the 19th century extended the scope of republican freedom through territorial expansion and admission of new states into the Union. At mid-century, amidst legal controversy over the nature of the Union and sectional conflict over slavery in republican society, they summoned the resources of constitutional conviction and moral purpose required to defend the constitutional rule of law against the claim of state secession. When advocates of secession used military force to pursue their goal, the federal government called out the military power of the Constitution to preserve the territorial and moral integrity of the Union.

In the course of the Civil War, the requirements of both military necessity and natural justice initiated the process of slave emancipation. Subsequently, the Reconstruction constitutional amendments secured the liberty and civil rights of emancipated slaves, rendering legally enforceable in all of the states the nation's founding principles of liberty, equality, and republican consent.

In the turbulent conditions produced by industrial expansion and social modernization in the late 19th century and early 20th century, the American people faced a different kind of constitutional challenge. Disaffected Progressive reformers, rejecting the limited-government constitutional ethos of the Founding, sought to establish economic regulatory and social welfare institutions based on a European model of centralized bureaucratic and collectivist government. Through strained and disingenuous interpretation of the Constitution, Progressive lawmakers and judges significantly reduced the sphere of individual liberty and property rights and expanded the scope of government regulation.

Threats to national security posed by totalitarian political movements in Germany and Russia in the 1930s inspired a strong sense of national unity and renewed appreciation for the American constitutional tradition. The experience of fighting World War II and the Cold War provided a grim reminder that the cause of liberty under the rule of law has always to be won anew against tyrannies of force and violence in changing historical circumstances.

Meanwhile, class-based domestic policy conflict encouraged by the Progressive movement was for a generation superseded as the principal focus of constitutional law and politics.

In the 1960s, a new cohort of liberals and radicals, under the pretext of the Vietnam War, resumed the Progressive attack on American constitutionalism. Although this attack continued after the end of the Cold War, the rise of modern conservative politics made it more possible to engage basic questions of the constitutional legitimacy of the regulatory welfare state than had been the case in the heyday of New Deal liberalism.

Like the natural law principles that it embodies, the historical reality of the Founders' Constitution possesses rational intelligibility and practical authority that command the assent of reasonable minds. The emergence of original intent jurisprudence in the 1970s and 1980s as a critique of modern liberal legalism clarified and affirmed the assumptions on which American constitutional orthodoxy have rested from the very beginning. Originalism shifted the burden of proof to liberals to justify their repudiation of the fundamental law of the Constitution in the name of the "living Constitution." Try as they might, liberal theorists were unable convincingly to falsify or expunge the real meaning of the Constitution as the standard by which governmental legitimacy is measured in the United States.

Considered from the standpoint of republican citizenship, American constitutionalism insists on fidelity to the text of the written fundamental law. It does so not in the belief that words are things that by their own force are capable of controlling the acts of government officials. What faithful republican citizens believe and understand, rather, is that the Constitution is the source of legitimate public authority: It expresses the deliberate will of the people under the rule of law, and it is required for the preservation of individual liberty and social freedom in self-governing political communities.

Chapter 1

ORIGIN OF THE CONSTITUTION IN THE ERA OF THE AMERICAN REVOLUTION

*T*he framing and ratification of the Constitution marked the culmination of the American Revolution against British imperial rule. In declaring national independence, the American colonists affirmed for themselves the natural rights and liberties that they had claimed as British subjects under the English common law. In separating themselves from the British nation, however, it was politically necessary for the American people to distinguish the constitutional authority by which they would govern themselves from that which they rejected.

The most important difference lay in the American conviction, acquired through the experience of colonial government as well as the revolutionary struggle, that a constitution was a written instrument promulgated by the authority of the people as the supreme law of the land. Its purpose was to define and establish in fixed form the principles, institutions, and rules of government. By contrast, the English idea of a constitution, arising out of feudal and aristocratic society, was of an assemblage of historically defined customs, practices, and institutions embodying basic national values. From the outset, the American commitment to text-based written constitutionalism was intended to hold government accountable to fundamental law in a practicable way that would facilitate deliberative government and discourage theoretical speculation.

Historically, a difference in outward form notwithstanding, the English and American constitutions have served the same basic purpose. A constitution is an ordering and account of the ways and means by which the people establish government power and provide for limitation in the exercise of that power, consistent with the ends and purposes that define their existence as a political community. To the extent that a constitution identifies the principles and objects of political life, it gives direction to the decisions and acts of public-spirited citizens and their representatives to the end of the common good of the community as well as their individual good. In a stronger sense implying legal sanction, a constitution determines the structures, forms, and procedures by which governmental power in a community is organized and exercised. Tension between these dimensions of constitutional meaning—that is, between standards of justice and right in the political community on the one hand and rules limiting the exercise of government power on the other—is reflected in controversy over the determination of constitutional meaning in particular situations.

While disavowing allegiance to the British nation, Americans, in constituting themselves as an independent people, were influenced by the history of English government and the Western political tradition of which it was a part. More so than in other world civilizations, Western thought from ancient to medieval times was concerned with the proper balance between freedom and authority in political life. Given the necessity of social order for human well-being, the practical problem was to establish systems of rule in constructive and responsible ways within defined institutional structures and legal constraints.

In Western civilization, two basic approaches to the problem of limited government evolved. The first was to organize and arrange the parts of government in a manner reflecting the composition of the community or society to the end that power be exercised with wisdom and moderation. In pre-modern times, the concept of mixed government, in which the social orders of kingship, aristocracy, and democracy were each recognized as having a role in the conduct of government, illustrated this approach to balance and limitation in the exercise of power. In the modern era, dating from the American Revolution, the idea of the separation of powers has been the dominant model for achieving constitutional limitation through the distribution and arrangement of institutions. In this approach, government is conceived in terms of distinct legislative, executive, and judicial functions rather than the mixing of social orders in the conduct of government.

The second rationale of constitutional limitation in Western political thought was premised on the idea of fundamental or higher law. In this approach, human agency is understood to be subject to order and direction by divine or natural law. The existence of political institutions and the power they exercise requires justification and legitimation according to the measure of external standards of justice and right, which possess superior moral and legal authority by virtue of their origin in the fundamental law of God or nature.

The practical expression of "higher-law" constitutionalism is the idea that government, like the society over which it exercises authority, is subject to the rule of law. In medieval England, common-law courts defined a body of law and legal right, outside the sphere of the king's prerogative, which protected the liberty and property rights of individual subjects against denial or deprivation by royal authority. Judicial specification of rules of adjudication based on principles of reason and justice enabled the common law to present itself as a kind of fundamental law.

The struggle between King and Parliament in the 17th century for control over English government raised the possibility that the common law might be recognized as a form of fundamental law limiting the supreme power of Parliament. The Revolution of 1688, signifying parliamentary victory over the Crown in the struggle for governmental sovereignty, precluded any such development. Ironically, the idea of a paramount constitutional law was to be transmitted and cultivated in more favorable historical and political circumstances through the settlement of colonies in North America during the same period of domestic political turmoil in England.

The moral and material elements for the design of the U.S. Constitution derived from the settlement of the American colonies. This obscure and unheralded extension of English political influence was based to a considerable extent on written, constitution-like documents of government foundation. Joint stock charters and feudal proprietary land grants, issued under royal authority, conferred powers on particular groups and persons to establish civil and political society, including economic enterprise.

As the earliest settlements became established, American colonists adopted new agreements, ordinances, and frames of government in a gradual extension of political organization into the interior of the continent. In the course of territorial settlement, the idea of republican government based on popular consent was practiced and conceptualized. Local self-government developed in a forthright republican manner in communities based on Protestant Reformation theology. The Massachusetts Bay Colony, legally organized under a joint stock corporation charter, was also a covenantal community of Puritan dissenters in the Church of England. Reflecting the separatist spirit of the Reformation, the colonies of Rhode Island and Connecticut were self-governing politico-religious associations formed from the fabric of Massachusetts Bay Puritanism.

With the exception of a brief period in the late 17th century when the Crown revoked charters and tried to impose a military government, the colonies enjoyed a substantial degree of autonomy in a mercantilist system of empire. England was concerned with commercial regulation of its North American and Caribbean colonies. Left largely to their own resources, the colonists evolved government institutions, legal systems, and political assumptions that by 1760 formed an inexplicit and unwritten American colonial constitution. Without in any conscious way rejecting the English political tradition, the colonists built up a body of institutional and intellectual experience on the basis of which principles of a distinctive form of constitutionalism were articulated in the crisis of the American Revolution.

Intrinsic to the settlement of the colonies was government by popular will based on republican representation and consent. This was the first principle of American constitutionalism. The circumstances of early settlement were such that representative institutions, involving the people in an active participant role and securing their cooperation and support by taking into account their rights and interests, was a practical requirement of colonial foundation. Although not democratic by modern standards, early American government was more pluralistic and effectively representational than English and European government of the time.

The contentious and factional nature of colonial politics gave rise to the separation of powers, a second basic constitutional principle. Colonial assemblies represented local constituents. In most of the colonies, the governor and council were appointed by royal authority. Conflicts of policy and interest between the two sources of authority caused legislative and executive powers to be exercised by different governmental agents in physically separated institutional settings rather than jointly as in the English mixed government scheme of King-in-Parliament. The growth of assembly power separate and distinct from that of the colonial governors provided the deposit of practical experience that was conceptualized in the separation of powers principle in the Revolution.

The federal principle of divided government sovereignty was a third constitutional principle rooted in the practices of colonial government. Abstractly considered, colonies are by definition political bodies dependent upon superior authority. In contrast, the American colonies, by virtue of the circumstances of their original settlement and the decentralized character of English mercantilist regulation, were able to exercise substantial authority in matters of internal government and society. Through the enactment of legislation concerning taxation, land distribution, economic activity, religion, the administration of justice, and social order in general, the colonies grew accustomed to a degree of autonomy that they believed was their rightful authority under the original charters and documents of foundation. At the same time, they acknowledged the power of Parliament to regulate trade within the British empire.

Without quite realizing it, in establishing institutions of local liberty the colonists questioned the assumption of unitary sovereignty on which the English constitution rested. Considered separately or individually, the colonies were parts of the British nation as a whole. With respect to internal political and social affairs, however, the particular rights, interests, and political needs of the colonies were so different from those of England as to warrant recognition of a distinct claim of internal sovereignty as a matter of constitutional right. The course of imperial policy from 1763 to 1776, intended to reduce the colonists to a status of complete dependency, instead convinced them that they were in fact no longer parts of Great Britain. As defenders of American liberty, they were parts of a new nation, the United States of America. From the experience of a practical division of sovereignty in the empire, Americans were prepared to adopt federalism as a basic principle of national constitutional identity.

For more than a decade, Americans protested a new imperial policy based on taxation without representation and consisting of measures designed to impose centralized control of colonial government and politics. In the opinion of the colonists, the policy violated individual liberty and property rights, both under their charters and frames of government and as loyal English subjects under the constitution of the empire. The decision to declare American independence in 1776 signified rebellion and revolution. Practically as well as logically, the decision required the establishment of new constitutional authority in colonies that were transformed into republican states joined in a national union to defend American liberty. To clarify, confirm, and actualize the new political reality, Americans proceeded to write compacts of fundamental law for their states and for the country as a whole.

Revolutionary constitution-making in America illustrated the appeal to higher law as the basis of political order. A new kind of American constitutionalism rested on the conviction, expressed by the Massachusetts House of Representatives in 1768, that "in all free states, the constitution is fixed," and neither legislative nor executive powers "can break through the fundamental rules of the constitution, without destroying their own foundation."[2] The idea of a paramount political law, given practicable effect in an intelligible text intended to limit the exercise of sovereign authority, thus emerged as the fourth and most fundamental principle of American constitutionalism.

The decision to ground American nationality in written fundamental law was based more on practical reason than on political theory. It seemed obvious that the ends of political society and security of personal liberty and property rights were better achieved by establishing objective constitutional limits on government rather than relying on an American parallel to an unstipulated and inexplicit arrangement of institutions and practices on the English model. The latter, in American experience, failed to limit government; in reality, it was not a true constitution. Americans believed that principles and rules essential to the exercise of public authority for the common good and the preservation of republican freedom should be separated from government and established in the form of fixed and objective standards.

Constitution-making reflected the political moderation of the American Revolution as an amalgam of tradition and innovation. Americans built on, rather than repudiated, their colonial past. They were concerned with maintaining the proper balance between liberty and authority under the natural law and divine providence, not with radical reconstruction of society according to visionary utopian aspiration. The proud claim, inscribed in the seal of the United States, that America

---

2. Address of the Massachusetts House of Representatives to Dennys de Berdt, Governor of Massachusetts, January 12, 1768.

was a "new order of the ages" (*Novus Ordo Seclorum*) referred to the ascendancy of the republican principle over the old order of monarchy and aristocracy.

Taken altogether, state constitution-making from 1776 to 1786 can be viewed as the creation of a kind of territorially distributed functional constitution for the country as a whole. Republican governments were organized on the separation of powers principle. State legislatures responsive to a broad electorate enacted policies concerning land, trade, taxation, and creditor–debtor relations. The governor's executive power, significantly reduced from that of colonial governors, was separated from lawmaking authority and confined to administrative duties. Courts and judicial officers conducted the administration of justice on the basis of statutes and common-law rules adapted to local circumstances. At the county and township levels, magistrates performed a variety of legal and political functions.

The states were the center of political attention and constitutional controversy because no government of genuine power and authority existed at the national level. The Continental Congress was formed in 1774 as a coordinating body of colonial delegates to recommend policy measures to the colonial assemblies. After the war for American independence began, Congress functioned largely in an advisory capacity. Its recommendations were subject to veto by state legislatures claiming to exercise independent sovereignty in light of their particular rights, interests, and political needs.

Nevertheless, immediate strategic and long-term geopolitical needs required some kind of general government for the nation that would be distinct from those of the states. Although formed by the states and consisting of state-appointed delegates, Congress, through its role as a coordinating body, was responsible for directing military and political policy for the country as a whole. To give it the authority needed to perform duties imposed by the wartime crisis, Congress drafted Articles of Confederation and Perpetual Union between the United States of America. This was a document of constitutional foundation at the national level analogous to the state constitutions at the local level.

During the Revolutionary War, opposition to centralized government was an obvious and justifiable concern. In congressional debate over the framing of the Articles of Confederation, therefore, partisans of states' rights were reluctant to give Congress the powers needed to transform it into a government of genuine republican authority. For example, Congress rejected a proposal permitting the exercise of state powers in all matters not interfering with the Articles of Confederation, which would have served as a standard against which to measure the legitimacy of state acts. Instead, states' rights delegates underscored the retention of state sovereignty. Article II declared: "Each state retains its sovereignty, freedom, and independence, and every Power, Jurisdiction, and right, which is not by this confederation expressly delegated to the United States, in Congress assembled."

Although it could be argued that Congress implicitly had the means necessary to carry out the functions assigned to it, failure to spell out legally coercive national powers proved an insuperable obstacle to stable and effective government. The Articles of Confederation were constitutionally defective because they did not confer the power to make and enforce law that is essential to government. Congress was limited to adopting resolutions and recommendations, mere requests that the states could ignore with impunity. A related weakness of the Confederation was the lack of a system of direct popular representation. Delegates to Congress were appointed by the state legislatures, and amendment of the Articles required approval by Congress and unanimous confirmation by the state legislatures.

It is important to note that, according to 18th century political science, a confederation as a form of political association was not intended to rest on a popular basis. In the circumstances of American society, however, the lack of popular representation was a defect. Americans thought of themselves as a national people, presumably destined to exist into the future. The idea of permanent nationality was expressed in a provision in the Articles of Confederation stating that the Articles "shall be inviolably observed by every State, and the Union shall be perpetual." Nevertheless, although a kind of national political debate took place in Congress, the constitutional structure of the Confederation did not encourage or sustain it. Without a basis in national popular sovereignty, the authority of the Confederation was unequal to that of the states. It was too readily subject to question by the state legislatures and perhaps incapable of summoning the material and political resources needed to maintain American national independence.

The adequacy of the Articles of Confederation to the demands of national union was the dominant issue in American politics in the 1780s. During the revolutionary crisis, union of the states was necessary to achieve independence from Great Britain; but while its continuation might be presumed, the nature and character of the Union in the absence of military exigency became a matter of dispute. Considered separately, the states had distinctive needs and interests involving liberty and property rights, debtor–creditor relations, and social order and stability that can be thought of as a kind of internal security requirement. Considered collectively, the United States had external security needs involving defense against aggression, diplomatic relations with other nations, and commercial exchange to promote American material prosperity. The question was whether, under the Articles of Confederation, the states were sufficiently consolidated and integrated in a constitutional sense to make possible the determination of rational and effective policies to meet the nation's internal and external security needs.

A nation—especially a self-governing republican nation— requires fixed constitutional procedures for making and executing deliberative judgments concerning the public interest and common good. On several occasions in the 1780s, Congress adopted proposals to remedy the lack of authority in the Confederation with respect to financial, commercial, and national defense matters. However, the constitutional requirement of unanimous state approval of changes in the Articles of Confederation proved an insuperable obstacle to effective governmental reform. As a practical political matter, therefore, the perception took hold that in order to strengthen the Confederation as a form of national government, the Articles of Confederation, in significant respects, would have to be replaced.

The framing and ratification of the Constitution consolidated, carried forward, and made permanent the results of the American Revolution. Contrary to the discredited contention of 20th century progressive historians, the Constitution was not a reactionary anti-democratic document. The principal object of the Revolution was to establish free society and national republican government in America. Destabilizing political conflict in the states, joined with an emerging consensus on the need to strengthen the authority of the Confederation, persuaded Congress to recommend and the states to appoint delegates to a convention held in Philadelphia in May 1787. The object of the Convention, as described by congressional resolution, was to report such alterations in the Articles of Confederation as would "render the federal constitution adequate to the exigencies of Government and the preservation of the Union."

The Convention dealt with the country's practical needs by making key constitutional revisions that authorized the Union government to enact policies beneficial to all the states. Specific policy needs included national revenue, national defense, economic development, and regulation of commerce among the states. The key constitutional changes were:

- To give Congress power to legislate for individuals in the states rather than request state governments to comply with congressional recommendations;
- To reconstitute the Union as a federal republic based on direct popular representation in the House of Representatives and equal state representation in the Senate;
- To organize the government of the Union as a legislative–executive–judicial separation of powers system rather than as a confederation of sovereign states; and
- To withdraw certain powers from the states while allowing them to retain substantial powers in the government of local affairs.

The Constitution did not abolish the states or reduce them to mere administrative districts dependent on the national government, as advocates of state sovereignty charged at the time. The Framers created "a more perfect Union" in the sense of extending the republican principle of the Revolution from the state level into the constitutional structure of government at the national level. The Founders "perfected" the Union—that is, brought it to a state or condition of greater fullness and completion—by making it more systematically republican. Establishment of the principle of direct popular representation was the key move that justified and legitimated the exercise of legislative sovereignty and legal coercion over individual persons by national legislative, executive, and judicial officers.

A new system of republican government was created at the national level for general purposes, corresponding to the separate systems of republican government that existed at the state level for local purposes. The government of the United States was superior to the state governments in the sense that, when exercising powers conferred by the Constitution in pursuance of national objects, acts of the national government were "the supreme law of the land." By the same token, powers not delegated to the United States by the Constitution, nor prohibited by it to the states, were reserved to the states or to the people. In this way, the Framers proposed to solve the problem of sovereignty that lay at the root of the constitutional controversy leading to the Revolution.

Rejecting the idea that sovereignty was unitary and indivisible, the Framers recognized the people of the United States as the sovereign constituent power of the nation as a whole. By determination of the popular will, expressed in the framing and ratification of the Constitution, government sovereignty was either delegated to the national government or reserved to the states. Federal and state governments had authority to legislate for and govern the same people in the same territory.

The difference between the two kinds of government— the one national and general, the other particular and local— lay in the purposes assigned to each. The definition of federalism as a form of political organization changed from its earlier meaning as a treaty alliance of sovereign states to that of a federal republican national Union. American federalism was a compound system of government combining elements of both a confederation of states and a nation of individual persons.

The Constitution transformed the revolutionary principles of federalism and republicanism into a system of national
authority. Ultimately, the Founders' greatest accomplishment,
making possible the perpetuation of American nationality
based on federal republican values, was to give practical expression to the idea of the Constitution as fundamental law. This
meant that the Constitution was distinguished from the institutions of government that it established and on which legal
limitations were imposed. The Constitution in this sense was a
paramount or higher law against which the legitimacy of government acts was measured.

As a foundational document, the Constitution was similar
to the state constitutions in positing a framework of government institutions. At a deeper level, the achievement of the
Framers transcended that of the state constitution-makers.
Delegates to the Constitutional Convention saw that the issue
facing them was not the construction of an original social contract community, as state constitution-makers conceived their
task. The Framers' concern was not with the protection of
natural rights in an original sense, but with the rights of individuals as modified by society and interwoven with the rights
of the states. The problem was not to eliminate or drastically
reduce the powers of the states, but to integrate the states and
the people into a deliberative national republican union without sacrificing the blessings of local republican liberty.

As a matter of historical fact and political self-under-
standing, the people and states of America were a nation. Yet
under the Articles of Confederation, the form of the nation
was constitutionally ambiguous or indeterminate. In the rational and deliberative sense required by republican government,
the nation under the Articles was unrepublican. The constituent parts were too loosely related and independent of each
other to act as a political community. The Framers' design for

a "more perfect Union" provided the degree of consolidation needed to constitute the parts of the nation into an effective whole, capable of taking its place in the emerging modern world of nation-states.

Faithful to the spirit and purpose of the Revolution, the Constitution expressed the character of a nation founded more on the republican principles of the Declaration of Independence than on historically received traditions of local community consensus. The Preamble identified the country's unifying ends and objects—the blessings of liberty, justice, domestic peace, the common defense, and general welfare—after which virtually the entire document was devoted to the practical design of forms, procedures, and institutions of government. As a form of fundamental law, the Constitution was less a covenant or compact for an integral, historically defined community than a contract-like specification of powers, duties, rights, responsibilities, and rules of government for the diverse people and communities that constituted the American Union.

Chapter 2

ELEMENTS OF
CONSTITUTIONAL POLITICS

*T*he nature of the Constitution as written fundamental
law raised a novel problem in the maintenance and
preservation of public law. In the English political tradition,
no real distinction existed between acts based on principled
adherence to the unwritten constitution on the one hand and
regular legislative acts based on political interests and ideology
on the other. By contrast, in the American system of written
fundamental law, the Constitution existed as an objective and
impartial expression of popular will and judgment, directed to
the common good of the nation and superior to government.
Nevertheless, and perhaps problematically, the nature of the
Constitution as a body of rules for the exercise of power in a
practical sense placed responsibility for its enforcement in the
first place on the government officers whom it was intended to
control.

In the new type of republican politics that developed after
ratification, public policy was conceived in relation to provisions of the constitutional text. If the maxims of republican
liberty were embodied in the document, fidelity to the text was
the measure of legitimacy in governmental practice. In a pluralistic, free society, however, partisanship, ideology, self-inter-

est, and political expediency were inevitable influences on government. Unless taken into account and brought under restraint, these forces threatened to reduce reference to the Constitution to a rhetorical formality. Invoking the constitutional document might serve as a pretext or justification for political action divorced from the principles and values of limited republican government.

In the view of the Founders, attachment to the Constitution was an achievement of reflection and practical reason. The force and effect of the Constitution as paramount law could not be left to the people's innate tendency toward law-abiding behavior.

During the ratification debate, James Madison discussed maintenance of the Constitution through arrangement and distribution of the parts of government, one of the two basic approaches to constitutionalism adopted by the Founders. In *Federalist* No. 51, Madison wrote that in framing a government, "You must enable the government to control the governed, and in the next place, oblige it to control itself." A dependence on the people was the primary control of government, "but experience has taught mankind the necessity of auxiliary precautions." To preserve liberty, it was necessary to prevent a concentration of powers in the same department. This was best accomplished by "giving to those who administer each department the necessary constitutional means, and personal motives, to resist the encroachments of the others.... Ambition must be made to counteract ambition. The interest of the man must be connected with the constitutional rights of the place."[3]

---

3. *Federalist* No. 51, in Alexander Hamilton, James Madison, John Jay [Publius], *The Federalist Papers* (New York: Penguin Group, 1961), pp. 321–322. Subsequent references to *The Federalist* cite essay and page number in this edition.

Giving illustration to the realism and practical reason of the Constitution, Madison observed: "This policy of supplying by opposite and rival interests, the defect of better motives, might be traced through the whole system of human affairs, private as well as public." The aim was "to divide and arrange the several offices in such a manner as that each may be a check on the other; that the private interest of every individual, may be a sentinel over the public rights."[4]

The Framers' realistic view of human nature was compatible with a sense of idealism, rightly understood. What enables constitutionalism to have a practical effect on political life, raising it above the level of cynicism on the one hand and incantation on the other, is moral and philosophical conviction. Attachment to the Constitution is based on the belief that the Constitution is good in itself, that its value is not simply instrumental. When citizens and government officials internalize constitutional principles and rules, acknowledging the intrinsic validity of the principles rather than their functional utility, they form convictions that give direction to political action. In this way, the Constitution has a configurative effect on political life.

Groups and individuals choose courses of action that they believe are consistent with or required by the Constitution. They do so not necessarily because in each instance they are philosophically committed to the particular constitutional principle at issue. In different circumstances, prudential considerations may point to another constitutional principle as the ground of action. In general, the issue is not the degree of subjective commitment with which a constitutional argument is made, but the fact that for the American people the Constitution is paramount and binding law. They believe it embodies

---

4. *Federalist* No. 51, p. 322.

the fundamental principles, forms, and procedures that are the measure of political and governmental legitimacy. Americans venerate the Constitution, and with good reason. Political actors and government officials take this fact into account and are constrained to act in conformity with the provisions of the fundamental law.

Although the Constitution presents itself in the form of positive law, it is erroneous to think that constitutionalism can be reduced to legal positivism: the belief that law is strictly empirical, consisting of nothing but the specific words posited by the promulgator of the law. On this view, constitutional interpretation becomes an exercise in semantic analysis.

At the same time, it is important to note that recognition of the higher-law nature of the Constitution in a sense points beyond the document to the principles embodied in it. From this circumstance, an opposite and equally serious misunderstanding of constitutionalism can result; namely, the tendency to disregard the plain meaning of the text in favor of speculative and ideologically driven constitutional interpretation. In the 20th century, various schools of progressive legal commentary used this methodology to argue for a "living Constitution" as an alternative to the Framers' Constitution.

The Founders cautioned against speculative construction outside the meaning and intent of the Constitution. Discussing two key provisions—the Necessary and Proper Clause and the Supremacy Clause—Alexander Hamilton wrote during the ratification debate:

> [I]t may be affirmed with perfect confidence that the constitutional operation of the intended government would be precisely the same if these clauses were entirely obliterated as if they were repeated in every article. They are only declaratory of a truth which would have resulted

by necessary and unavoidable implication from the very act of constituting a federal government and vesting it with certain specific powers.[5]

If the text of the Constitution was in some respects declaratory of the truths of political philosophy or the science of government, as Hamilton argued, in what sense was it essential? The answer is that it was a requirement of constitutional practical reason. Hamilton said that the Necessary and Proper Clause was written into the Constitution as a precaution "to guard against all caviling refinements in those [state government officials] who might hereafter feel a disposition to curtail and evade the legitimate authorities of the Union." On this and other key points, Hamilton observed, the Convention thought it best "to leave nothing to construction."[6]

The decision to adopt a written constitution was intended to build the rule of law into the structure of political government, substituting peaceful constitutional change for violent revolutionary upheaval. The question facing the American people, Hamilton wrote in *Federalist* No. 1, was "whether societies of men are really capable or not, of establishing good government from reflection and choice, or whether they are forever destined to depend, for their political constitutions, on accident and force."[7] This was not a utopian vision of conflict-free communitarian politics as advocated by Anti-Federalist critics of the Constitution. The "more perfect Union" envisioned by the Founders was a realistic design for energetic and limited government based on the informed will and judgment of the American people as a whole.

---

5. *Federalist* No. 33, p. 202.
6. *Ibid.*, p. 203.
7. *Federalist* No. 1, p. 33.

The Founders created a complex government of delegated and dispersed, yet articulated and balanced, powers based on the principle of consent. The consent principle was in turn affirmed in the constitutional requirement of cooperation and concurrence among the branches of government for the conduct of public business. Made for an open, acquisitive, individualistic, and pluralistic society, the Constitution ordered the diverse constituent elements of American politics. More than merely a neutral procedural instrument for registering the movement of social forces, it was a statement of ends and means for maintaining the principles that defined Americans as a national people.

Madison observed in *Federalist* No. 10 that the intent of the Framers was to supply "a republican remedy for the diseases most incident to republican government."[8] The Constitution assumed the status of fundamental and higher law because it expressed the will of the people, but was popular self-government really something more than a rhetorical figure of speech? Were the people in a collective sense truly capable of exercising the powers of government? If they were, could government by the popular sovereign actually be subjected to constitutional limitations? Considering that the people of the United States were also constituents of the several states claiming reserved constitutional powers, it was pertinent to ask further whether state sovereignty, justified in the name of popular sovereignty, might threaten the Constitution's design of limited republican government.

To raise these questions is not anti-democratic or elitist, as Anti-Federalist opponents of the Constitution charged. The first point to establish in understanding the republican character of the Founding is precisely that recognition of the people

---

8. *Federalist* No. 10, p. 84.

as the constituent sovereign is not inconsistent with reasonable limitations on the power of the people. Ratification of the Constitution by popular conventions was in fact an acknowledgment of the wisdom and practicability of placing institutional restraints on popular sovereignty.

Madison noted in *Federalist* No. 10 that in a pure democracy, the people assemble and govern in person or directly. In a republic, by contrast, representatives are chosen by the people to govern on their behalf. The strength of the idea of democratic equality is such, however, that in a representative democracy as well as in a direct democracy, there is a sense in which, as the philosopher Yves Simon observes, "the people retains the character of a deliberating assembly."[9]

From this we can infer the existence of an informal feature in American constitutionalism that expresses the spirit of direct democracy. This feature is the power of public opinion. Although the constitutionally mandated electoral process may be viewed as the only legitimate source of public opinion, it is very difficult to confine the concept to this institutional form. In a system where the will of the people is considered paramount, there are strong incentives to extend the scope of public opinion into a variety of forms of social and cultural communication.

The Framers thus recognized the ascendancy of the popular will and made provision for responsibility and moderation in its exercise. In the dialectic between freedom and authority in American constitutionalism, government derives its legitimate powers from the popular sovereign on the one hand, while institutional arrangements qualify and refine the opinions and will of the people on the other.

---

9.   Yves R. Simon, *Philosophy of Democratic Government* (Notre Dame, Ind.: University of Notre Dame Press, 1993), p. 186.

The most significant limitations on popular sovereignty are based on the principles of federalism, the separation of powers, and the Constitution as fundamental law. Of these, the distinctive excellence of the Constitution consists in its status as supreme law of the land. Closely, if not inseparably, related to the Constitution as supreme law is the practice of judicial review, by which courts preserve limitations on the legislative power that the Framers believed are "essential in a limited constitution."[10]

The United States is exceptional among modern nations in the constitutional continuity and stability that it has enjoyed over the span of two centuries. Continuity has been sustained not by defiant resistance to change, but through timely development of basic constitutional principles in changing historical circumstances.

Consider, for example, the constituent sovereignty of the people and republican consent. It might be thought that the way to preserve and improve a democratic republic is to make it ever more democratic. To be sure, populist arguments have been made calling for centralization of power under the rule of direct democracy, but these demands have been resisted through development of republican popular sovereignty as conceived by the Founders in systematic conjunction with the principles of federalism, the separation of powers, and the Constitution as fundamental law. The practical reason of the Constitution, by which the rights of the people and powers of government are so distributed and balanced as to achieve a deliberative national majority, thus permits subsequent genera-tions of Americans to participate, as it were, in the mind of the Founders.

---

10. *Federalist* No. 78, p. 466.

To appreciate the Framers' achievement, it is pertinent to note a key distinction between ancient and modern constitutional thinking. In ancient political thought, a constitution was equated with the way of life of a people or community. In modern thought, a constitution is narrowly defined in terms of the forms, procedures, and institutions of government and politics. We may think of the Constitution in a broad sense as symbolic of our national character, but we don't turn to it as an account of our way of life. The Constitution is an instrument of government and fundamental law that illustrates a distinctive form of practical political action. When we refer to the United States Constitution as fundamental law, we mean that it sets the standard by which political and governmental legitimacy are evaluated and determined.

More specifically, the Constitution brings together in a variety of institutional settings the respective purposes and concerns of law and politics as modes of authority essential to republican government. Politics influences or controls government, and government needs law to maintain social order and promote the common good. In an ideal sense, the rule of law aims at impartial and universal justice. Precise, clearly defined, general, and prospective, it transcends and requires autonomy from direct political control. Political rule is concerned with practical judgments of right action in particular circumstances. Influenced by a multitude of contingent interests and demands, it is by nature discretionary and result-oriented. In a rightly ordered constitutional government, politics and law need to be distinguished from each other without being categorically divorced.

In the colonial and revolutionary era, politics was carried on in relative detachment from law by factions formed on the basis of economic, social, ethnic, and religious identities and interests. In *Federalist* No. 10, Madison argued that the extended national republican government proposed in the Constitution was the best way to limit the influence of faction in the states, which he believed was the main source of the weakness and instability of the Confederation. Madison defined faction as a minority or a majority of citizens "united and actuated by a common impulse of passion or interest adverse to the rights of other citizens or to the permanent and aggregate interests of the community."[11]

Ratification of the Constitution brought about a new approach to government based on the formation of political parties. Pre-constitutional factional politics was informally organized around local elites on an issue-by-issue basis. Government and politics were carried on as a kind of personal and proprietary activity rather than as an impartial public thing that warranted the involvement, interest, and responsibility of the people as a whole. The irregular factions that characterized revolutionary and Confederation politics were superseded by more permanent political organizations. Parties were voluntary associations of citizens united by shared political sentiments and organized on the basis of permanent economic and social interests.

The requirements of aggregating public opinion and giving direction to national policy led to the formation in the 1790s of the Federalist Party under President George Washington and the Democratic Republican Party under Secretary of State Thomas Jefferson. Although not specifically envisioned by the Founders, the constitutional functions served by political parties were significant. It was necessary to mobilize and coordinate competing opinions and interests in republican society. There was a need to coordinate the separate branches of government created by the Constitution in order

---

11. *Federalist* No. 10, p. 78.

to conduct effective public policy and administration. In this sense, parties signified an extension of the principle of republican representation.

Furthermore, legislative proposals in Congress were justified in terms of constitutional principle and authority, as well as policy considerations. Policymaking was interwoven with and complicated by arguments over the correct interpretation or true understanding of the Constitution. This combination of purposes and functions is comprehended in the uniquely American concept and practice of "constitutional politics."

Political party identification presupposed constitutional fidelity and national loyalty. Permanent organized opposition to government was traditionally regarded as dangerous to the body politic and inherently seditious. In republican society, conflicts of rights, interests, and opinions were to be expected. Uniformity of opinion was not possible except at the cost of tyranny. For parties to be truly republican and constitutional, therefore, opinions and public policy recommendations attentive to the national interest had to be conceived broadly enough to represent the people as a whole.

Properly understood, party competition could serve the constitutional end of a more perfect Union not by eliminating opposing points of view, but by promoting reasoned deliberation about wise policies for the common good. If, on the other hand, loyalty to party became an end in itself, constitutional fidelity might be eroded and national union placed in jeopardy. The aggrandizing logic of partisan loyalty, ambition, and ideology posed a particular threat to the constitutional design of government power that was divided and dispersed to preserve individual and local liberty.

The concept of "constitutional politics" recognizes the significance of political partisanship in American constitutional development; but reasonable as the concept is, it con-

31

tains a potentially destabilizing ambiguity. In constitutional politics, political actors, including lawmakers, executive officers, and judges, advocate public policies for reasons of wisdom, expediency, and partisan and ideological advantage. They justify these policies by appealing to constitutional principles and requirements that they claim have the authority of public law. Political and legal considerations, in an ideal sense distinguished from each other, are intermingled, conflated, and confused. Motives are questioned and integrity is impugned amidst accusations of "playing politics" with the Constitution.

Unsavory though it may appear, in a free and pluralistic society, constitutional politics provides the context in which the principles of federalism, the separation of powers, and judicial review as the corollary of written fundamental law have been construed and developed. If political ideas are reduced to personal preference and politics is regarded as a purely self-interested and aggrandizing activity, the notion of constitutional politics as a means of constitutional preservation becomes contradictory and incoherent. If, however, we retain or recover the Founders' belief that principles of reason, justice, and right really exist and can be apprehended as guides to practical action by individual actors in virtue of their human nature, then constitutional preservation through the practice of constitutional politics is morally and intellectually justified.

In the 18th century, Americans were precocious in their constitutional self-education. Within a generation, principles that justified a revolution gained recognition as constitutional orthodoxy.

This is not to say, however, that constitutional differences of opinion did not occur. The Constitution was not a self-enforcing document the authority of which preempted or precluded dispute over its meaning. Constitutional questions, embedded in partisan, ideological, and policy considerations, were often highly contested. Their resolution in particular cases was rarely conclusive, given the right of dissenting opinion to appeal to the Constitution for reconsideration of a particular decision by legislative or judicial authority. Accordingly, the determination of constitutional orthodoxy was an ongoing developmental process that depended on construction of the basic structural principles of federalism, the separation of powers, and the scope of judicial review as a limitation on government power.

Chapter 3

FEDERALISM AND THE NATURE OF THE UNION

$\mathcal{T}$he nature of the Union was the central problem in American constitutional development from 1789 to 1860. In the ratification debate, James Madison, in *Federalist* No. 39, described the nature of the Union in terms of the principle of divided sovereignty. Madison's key idea was that the Union was partly federal and partly national in its structural and operational character. Its foundation was federal on account of its ratification by the people as forming many independent states rather than a single consolidated nation. The sources from which government powers derived were both national and federal: The people of America were represented in the House of Representatives, and the states were represented in the Senate. The executive power was derived from national and federal sources through the operation of the electoral college.

In its operation, the government of the Union was national, its laws being directed to individual citizens. In the extent of its powers, the Union was national and federal. Acts of Congress were supreme over objects lawfully assigned in the Constitution, and state and local authorities exercised "distinct and independent portions of the supremacy" in their respective spheres and "inviolable sovereignty" over objects not delegated to the United States.[12]

Madison further noted the creation of the Supreme Court of the United States as a tribunal to decide controversies between the jurisdictions of national and state governments. The existence of the Supreme Court, whose decisions were to be made impartially according to the rules of the Constitution, was in Madison's opinion "clearly essential to prevent an appeal to the sword, and a dissolution of the compact."[13]

Finally, the constitutional amending process, necessary to preservation of the Constitution should institutional practices reveal flaws in its design, was neither wholly federal nor wholly national. The requirement of approval by three-fourths of the states avoided determination either by a national majority on the one hand or by the rule of state unanimity on the other.

The main point was that the Constitution divided government sovereignty between the states and the national government. The Union was a compound of two distinct concepts of political association: the republican principle of popular consent, the inherent tendency of which was toward unity and consolidation of power, and the federal principle of compact tending toward plurality and dispersal of power. It was not obvious, however, that a nation could be constituted on two different principles of association or that, if so organized, it would not inevitably become all one thing or all the other. In the context of partisan and ideological competition, what would prevent supporters of national or state sovereignty from aggrandizing their power, each side at the expense of the other?

The principle of divided sovereignty was an insufficient motive for constitutional enforcement. Conflicting opinions

---

12. *Federalist* No. 39, p. 245.
13. *Ibid.*, p. 246.

were bound to arise over the respective powers of the national and state governments and over the locus of authority to decide such a constitutional dispute. The Constitution did not expressly designate a final arbiter of its meaning. There were reasonable grounds for claiming that the states or the national government or the people as constituent power possessed the authority to determine constitutional meaning. Insofar as the Constitution was a system of political institutions, the nature of the Union was a political question to be decided by the political branches of government. Insofar as the Constitution was the supreme law of the land, the nature of the Union could be viewed as a legal or juridical question to be decided by the judicial branch of government.

The practice of American politics in the 19th century gave rise to a concept of political action that provided a rule of constitutional fidelity. The rule held that neither the national government nor the states could rightly reduce the other to itself or otherwise destroy it. This was not a positive legal rule written into the Constitution, but an unwritten rule of constitutional practical reason evincing attachment to the federal republican ground of American nationality.

In the basic purpose of making "a more perfect Union," the Constitution and the Union were treated as equivalent terms having a reciprocally related and intertwined meaning. Like the original act of foundation, the preservation of the Union depended on or was subject to a political rule of reason. As between national ends and objects on the one hand and state and local ends and objects on the other, the Constitution gave priority to the former. The design of the Constitution was integrative and consolidating, not decentralizing and particularistic.

Most important, the practical reason of the Constitution made control of the national government the paramount goal of politics within the federal system. The right of the constitutional majority to exercise enumerated national powers for designated ends and objects was intrinsic to the idea of republican government.

The assertion of state sovereignty and states' rights, by contrast, was the default strategy of the electoral minority. The Kentucky and Virginia Resolutions of 1798, protesting the Sedition Act as unconstitutional, showed how states could resist measures of the national government that were believed to exceed constitutional limitations. By the same token, the national government on several occasions enforced laws against the acts of state officials and citizens that they believed violated the Constitution. Both constitutional constructions—"state interposition" against national usurpation of reserved state powers and "national interposition" against obstruction of federal authority—could be viewed as upholding the Constitution. The same arguments, however, could be viewed as a pretext for the pursuit of partisan and ideological purposes.

From 1789 to 1860, the nature of the Union as a constitutional question was implicated in political, economic, social, and territorial expansion policy conflicts. No agreement could be reached on any convincing and conclusive determination of the relative powers of the national and state governments. The partly federal, partly national division of government sovereignty, regulated by public opinion expressed in partisan electoral competition, permitted flexibility in policy responses within an accepted framework of constitutional legitimacy. In the major political conflicts that defined the growth of the country—most notably the Louisiana Purchase in 1803, the Missouri Compromise in 1820, the nullification crisis of 1833, and the Compromise of 1850—Constitution and Union were preserved. In situations where the threat of disunion presented itself, partisan opponents agreed to disagree for the sake of national unity.

Moderation was the price of Union, but the disposition to compromise was a contingent thing that depended on the issues about which Americans were willing to disagree. The economic interests involved in policy disputes concerning banks, tariffs, internal improvements, land distribution, and regulation of commerce were negotiable. In these matters, the nature of the Union with respect to the relative powers of the national and state governments was satisfactorily recognized in policy measures adopted by the Democrat and Whig parties. With respect to the republican element in the principle of federal republican Union, however, partisan and sectional interests proved more difficult to reconcile because the main issue in dispute was the meaning and significance of slavery in American society and its compatibility with the principle of republican freedom.

In addition to the problem of the relative powers of the federal and state governments, the slavery issue presented a question of moral choice concerning the meaning of American nationality. The Constitution recognized the existence of slavery in several states. It conferred on the institution a measure of protection in the form of the Fugitive Slave Clause, which provided for the return of escaped slaves; the Importation and Migration Clause, under which Congress could not prohibit the importation of slaves for a period of 20 years (until 1808); and the clause establishing the three-fifths ratio between slaves and free persons as the rule for apportioning representation in the House of Representatives and for direct taxation. In the view of the Founders, the meaning of these provisions was summed up in the proposition that freedom was national and slavery local. With the development of a full-fledged slave society in the 19th century, however, southerners argued that the Constitution established slavery as a national institution, protecting it from interference or impairment by antislavery advocates and partisans of free labor.

In the 1840s, the annexation of Texas into the Union and the acquisition of the California, Utah, and New Mexico territories from Mexico by military conquest reignited national controversy over slavery that had been quiescent since the Missouri Compromise of 1820. In territories acquired as a result of the Mexican War, both the North and the South claimed authority under the Constitution, either through congressional legislation or through a Supreme Court decision concerning slavery, to adopt a policy extending their particular conceptions of republican society and government into national territories.

Narrowly conceived, the constitutional issue concerned the locus of decision-making power: Where in the federal system—at the national, state, or territorial level of government—did the constitutional authority to determine the status of slavery in national territories lie?

The Constitution did not expressly answer this question. The most prominent theories proposed to resolve the controversy were the northern Democrat principle of territorial or popular sovereignty; the Republican and Free Soil commitment to exclusion of slavery from the territories by congressional legislation; and the South's insistence on the constitutional right of citizens to take their property—including slave property—into national territories. These several constitutional solutions to the territorial slavery question were woven into the Wilmot Proviso, the territorial legislation on Utah and New Mexico in the Compromise of 1850, the Kansas–Nebraska Act of 1854, the *Dred Scott* decision of 1857, and the party platforms in the election of 1860.

More broadly conceived, the constitutional issue posed by territorial slavery was whether the country could hold together in the face of mounting sectional hostility and a sense of impending conflict. Was the Founders' Constitution adequate to the political and governmental demands of an expanding and increasingly pluralistic society in which Americans' understanding of national identity and interest depended on their view of the slavery question? With the exception of extremists in both sections—"fire eaters" in the South and abolitionists in the North—neither side advocated disunion. Partisans in both sections claimed fidelity to the Constitution and the Union in the name of republican nationality. And in both sections, by the familiar if ambiguous logic of American constitutionalism, political motives and interests intersected with constitutional reasoning, argument, and interpretation.

When South Carolina seceded from the Union following the election of Abraham Lincoln as President in 1860, it might have been better to amend the Constitution in the hope of averting disunion and civil war. In fact, 57 resolutions proposing 200 constitutional amendments were introduced in Congress. Nevertheless, the timetable and institutional procedures established by the Constitution for the administration of the national government could not be suspended. At this point, the question of slavery in republican society was absorbed into or conflated with the problem of the nature of the Union.

Did a state, by virtue of its ratification of the Constitution or other claim of sovereign authority, have a constitutional or legal right to withdraw its ratification and resign its membership in the Union by adopting an ordinance of secession? Analogously, did the United States, acting through the agency of the national government, have constitutional authority to resist the secession movement? Again, the Constitution did not expressly answer these questions. Properly understood in the light of the intent of the Framers, the design of the Constitution, and the historical experience of federal republican government, however, the Constitution authorized resistance to secession as lawless and unjustified rebellion.

The secession crisis posed anew, and in a more threatening form, the fundamental issue faced in the formation of the Union: whether the people and states of America constituted a nation. To meet the crisis, Lincoln as chief executive exercised authority both conferred in Article II of the Constitution and grounded in the practical reason of national sovereignty as disclosed in the conduct of federal–state relations from 1789 to 1860. The record of practical administration under the Constitution showed that, despite conflicting opinions, the Union was not the indeterminate, voluntary compact between completely sovereign states that was claimed in secessionist theory. To the contrary, for constitutionally defined national purposes, the Union was a sovereign government constituted on the principles of divided government sovereignty and republican freedom.

No political party or executive administration ever regarded the Union as a political association dependent for its existence on the willingness of states and citizens, according to their subjective judgment and decision, to obey the Constitution and laws of the nation. Although political minorities had made threats of disunion, this did not prove the existence of a constitutional right of secession. The Union was the kind of political community and government that was not to be broken at will and with impunity. To serve the constitutional end of making "a more perfect Union," the interlocking system of powers and constraints between the national and state governments that defined the principle of federal republican Union required confirmation and preservation.

Lincoln's First Inaugural spelled out the constitutional issues at stake in the secession crisis. He declared that "the Union of these States" was "a government proper," which under the Constitution and in the light of "universal law" was intended to be perpetual. Like the "fundamental law of all national governments," there was no provision in the Constitution providing for the termination of the Union. If in pursuance of ordinances of secession acts of violence should be taken against the authority of the United States, the acts would be treated as insurrectionary or revolutionary. The laws of the Union would be faithfully executed in accordance with executive duty under the Constitution.

The practical reason of republican government precluded the claim of secession as the constitutional right of a minority. Lincoln said that no constitution could be framed with a provision applying to every question arising "in practical administration." The Constitution, for example, did not expressly say whether fugitive slaves should be returned by national or state authority or whether Congress could prohibit or was required to protect slavery in the territories. From such questions arose constitutional controversies that divided the country into majorities and minorities. "If the minority will not acquiesce, the majority must, or the government must cease. There is no other alternative; for continuing the government, is acquiescence on one side or the other." "Plainly," Lincoln declared, "the central idea of secession, is the essence of anarchy. A majority, held in restraint by constitutional checks, and limitations, and always changing easily, with deliberate changes of popular opinion, is the only true sovereign of a free people. Whoever rejects it, does, of necessity, fly to anarchy or to despotism."[14]

The Founders recognized war and rebellion as political conditions that the country might encounter. After the attack on Fort Sumter, therefore, no provision was made for the suspension of the Constitution and replacement of civil by military government. The conduct of the war nevertheless disclosed the existence, in time of national emergency, of justifiable exercises of presidential authority not otherwise sanctioned under the Constitution.

In his message to Congress on July 4, 1861, Lincoln justified and sought legislative approval for acts taken at the start of the war. He referred specifically to calling up the state militia into national service, ordering an increase in the size of the regular army, and suspending the writ of habeas corpus. The issue presented was whether, "in all republics," there was "this inherent and fatal weakness?" "Must a government, of necessity, be too *strong* for the liberties of its own people, or too *weak* to maintain its own existence?"

Lincoln made the constitutional determination that "no choice was left but to call out the war power of the Government; and so to resist force, employed for its destruction, by force for its preservation."[15] Referring to the writ of habeas corpus, in words that might as well have been written into the Constitution, Lincoln defended his action: "Are all the laws, *but one*, to go unexecuted, and the government itself go to pieces, lest that one be violated?" Denying that any law was violated, he cited as authority the text of the Constitution: "The privilege of the writ of habeas corpus, shall not be suspended unless when, in cases of rebellion or invasion, the public safety may require it." Noting the silence of the Constitution as to which branch of government had the power, Lincoln said that "it cannot be believed the framers of the

---

[14.] Abraham Lincoln, "First Inaugural Address," in *Lincoln: His Speeches and Writings*, p. 585.

[15.] Abraham Lincoln, "Message to Congress in Special Session," July 4, 1861, in *Lincoln: His Speeches and Writings*, p. 598.

instrument intended, that in every case, the danger should run its course" until Congress could convene to determine whether suspension of the writ was necessary.[16]

The continuation of constitutional politics, together with the special demands placed on the executive power, caused Lincoln's conduct of the war to be controversial. The element of military necessity in presidential decision making was conspicuous in relation to three issues in particular: internal security and civil liberties, slave emancipation, and the reconstruction of loyal governments in states coming under Union military control. Of these, slave emancipation was most salient in relation to the constitutional controversy over republican freedom and the nature of the Union that led to the war.

Secession produced a political and constitutional paradox that resisted logical resolution throughout the Civil War and Reconstruction era. From the Union point of view, southern disunion was a legal nullity that left the Union unbroken in a constitutional sense. On this theory, the seceded states, although lacking republican governments in the sense of the Constitution, were still members of the Union, and slavery, as a domestic local institution, was beyond the power of the national government to regulate or abolish.

In fact, however, the Union was disrupted, and the states were, in Lincoln's own words, "out of their proper practical relation with the Union." It was politically impossible, as well as unreasonable from the standpoint of executive duty, to recognize a sphere of immunity in which slavery was protected against the consequences of exercising military power for the preservation of the Union and the Constitution. Military emancipation was further warranted by the clause of the Con-

---

16. *Ibid.*, p. 601.

stitution providing that the United States "shall guarantee to every State in this Union a Republican Form of Government." Together, these considerations justified a policy of military emancipation in states specifically where the people were in rebellion against the United States.

The Emancipation Proclamation of January 1, 1863, declared that all persons held as slaves in states designated as being in rebellion "are, and henceforward shall be free." Lincoln's order stated that the "executive government" of the United States, including military and naval authorities, would "recognize and maintain the freedom of said persons," of whom those of suitable condition would be received into the military service of the United States to garrison forts and man vessels. Lincoln characterized emancipation as a measure that was "sincerely believed to be an act of justice, warranted by the Constitution, upon military necessity," upon which he invoked "the considerate judgment of mankind, and the gracious favor of Almighty God."

To the extent that it proceeded during the war, military emancipation was irreversible. It therefore established a political and moral commitment on the basis of which postwar constitutional amendments were enacted securing the results of the war. The constitutional significance of the war was two-fold. First, it confirmed the nature of the Union as a sovereign national government with authority to preserve the nation against unjustified rebellion. Second, it affirmed the right of black Americans to the protection of personal liberty, basic civil rights, and national citizenship. In this way it clarified and confirmed the nature of republican freedom and consent as principles of American nationality.

The Reconstruction amendments prohibited slavery and guaranteed basic civil and political rights of United States citizens. They did not expressly prohibit secession or recognize the power of the national government to preserve the Constitution and the Union. On these fundamental points of constitutional construction, the outcome of the war and the enactment of the amendments were facts that spoke for themselves.

The Reconstruction amendments, which authorized Congress to enforce their provisions by means of appropriate legislation, preserved the Constitution through the development and elaboration of principles of national foundation.

- The Thirteenth Amendment (1865) declared that neither slavery nor involuntary servitude shall exist in the United States or any place subject to their jurisdiction. The prohibition of slavery was national in scope, directed both to states and to private individuals.
- The Fourteenth Amendment (1868) clarified the nature and attributes of republican freedom. It conferred national and state citizenship on all persons born or naturalized in and subject to the jurisdiction of the United States. The amendment prohibited states from abridging the privileges and immunities of United States citizens; depriving persons of life, liberty, and property without due process of law; and denying persons the equal protection of the laws.
- The Fifteenth Amendment (1870) prohibited the national and state governments from denying United States citizens the right to vote on account of race, color, or previous condition of servitude.

By extending the sphere of republican freedom and by limiting the powers of the states with respect to personal liberty and civil rights, the Reconstruction amendments fulfilled the Founders' purpose of making a more perfect Union. As a settlement of the issues for which the war was fought, however, they met serious resistance in the form of southern public opinion. From the standpoint of southern and northern Democrats, the Reconstruction amendments were unconstitutional because they were framed by a Congress from which the seceded states were excluded, in violation of the principle of republican consent. If secession was the legal nullity that the Union theory of the war said it was, the former Confederate states had a constitutional right, in the opinion of southerners, to resume their standing in Congress upon the taking of an oath of loyalty.

For partisan, prudential, and morally justifiable reasons, the Republican majority that controlled Congress rejected this conclusion. In order to restore national unity while maintaining constitutional continuity in federal–state relations to the extent possible in conditions of civil disorder and violence, Congress in the Reconstruction Act of 1867 established provisional military governments to secure the ratification and enforcement of the Reconstruction amendments and the Civil Rights Act of 1866. Amidst widespread racial violence, under the protection of Union military authority augmented by additional civil rights enforcement acts in 1870 and 1871, southern state governments and constitutions acceptable to the Republican majority were organized and readmitted to Congress under the Guarantee of Republican Government Clause of the Constitution.

Unless federal military rule was to continue indefinitely, however, historical and cultural forces in the South favored the restoration of white political rule. Recognition of this fact influenced the violently contested election of 1876, which ended in an Electoral College stalemate. Congress appointed an Electoral Commission consisting of 10 Members of Congress and five Supreme Court judges to count the electoral votes. The commission decided in favor of Republican candidate Rutherford B. Hayes, who in an act of compromise subsequently withdrew federal troops from the South. Reconstruction thus ended, and white political rule was restored in the former Confederate states.

The Reconstruction amendments were nationally integrative in purpose and intent. Their adoption signified the preservation and development of the Founders' constitutional principles through constructive application in new political circumstances. The abolition of slavery and recognition of black Americans' personal liberty and civil rights extended the principle of republican freedom throughout the country as a whole. The result was to expand significantly the constitutional identity of the people of the United States, fulfilling the promise of the "new birth of freedom" heralded in Lincoln's Gettysburg Address in 1863. The expansion of republican freedom in turn necessitated a revision of federal–state relations in the direction of greater national authority over civil rights and liberties at the expense of the powers of the states.

Because of the contradictions it involved, Reconstruction has a mixed historical reputation. States' rights advocates past and present, as well as modern economic libertarians, have condemned it as a constitutional monstrosity. Civil rights activists have either lamented the failure to promote radical property redistribution in the South or viewed the Reconstruction amendments as a revolution in federalism giving the national government plenary authority over civil rights. The protection of civil and political rights on a racially impartial basis was a long and arduous undertaking that was not substantially achieved until the second half of the 20th century. Critics fail to appreciate, however, the beneficial effect of the Reconstruction amendments in balancing the integrative force of democratic republicanism with the decentralizing tendency of the federal division of sovereignty.

The end of Reconstruction signaled a reduction in political violence without which the Founders' project of republican constitutionalism probably could not have been sustained. Both parts of the reunited country could point to different events in the Civil War era that in their opinion signified the breakdown of constitutional government and the rule of law. These perceptions have had a lasting effect on American politics. Nevertheless, slavery was abolished, constitutional amendments necessary for the preservation of the Union were adopted, and the unwisdom and futility of secession as a political teaching and constitutional doctrine were exposed.

Meanwhile, the demands of commercial and industrial development, upon which national prosperity depended, raised constitutional and legal questions concerning the proper relationship between individual liberty and property rights and the public interest. Although similar to economic regulatory issues dealt with in the antebellum period, these questions took on a new aspect in relation to the Reconstruction amendments. The Fourteenth Amendment proved to be an especially fertile source of controversy in matters concerning economic liberty and property rights from the late 19th century until the middle of the 20th century.

Chapter 4

CONSTITUTIONAL DEVELOPMENT AND ECONOMIC MODERNIZATION

*A*merican constitutionalism underwent a gradual transformation following the Civil War. The problem of the nature of the Union that was intrinsic to the establishment of the Constitution as fundamental law was settled—at least for the foreseeable future. The nation's core federal republican identity was affirmed and revised in light of the natural rights principles of the Founding.

In new social conditions caused by the development of modern industrial production, the principles of the separation of powers and judicial review of the Constitution as fundamental law now assumed greater significance in government and politics. Grounded in the revolutionary and Constitution-making experience of the Founding era, both principles were integral to the structure of the Constitution. While not expressly described in the constitutional text, the separation of powers and judicial review were justified by the practical reason of the Constitution as a system of limited republican government. In the post-Reconstruction period, the role of the judiciary in government and politics changed more dramatically than the institutional relationship between Congress and the presidency under the separation of powers.

In the Founding era, both Federalists and Anti-Federalists recognized the role that courts might potentially play in enforcing the Constitution. In one sense, adherence to the fundamental law depended on the civic virtue and integrity of political actors accountable to the will of the people as the constituent power. In another sense, fidelity to the Constitution as the supreme law of the land provided warrant for, if it did not require, judicial oversight of legislative and executive acts for conformity with the Constitution.

In *Marbury v. Madison* (1803),[17] the Supreme Court for the first time exercised the power of judicial review. It affirmed the authority of federal courts to determine whether an act of Congress was legally valid when considered in relation to express provisions of the Constitution.

The statute in question was the Judiciary Act of 1789, defining the powers and duties of national courts. In a unanimous opinion, Chief Justice John Marshall found that the Act conferred jurisdiction on the Supreme Court outside the jurisdictional limits defined by Article III of the Constitution. Justifying the idea of judicial review, Marshall said that, on the theory of a written constitution, "an act of the legislature, repugnant to the Constitution, is void." Such an act did not bind and oblige a court to give it effect. Marshall further declared:

> It is, emphatically, the province and duty of the judicial department, to say what the law is.... So if a law be in opposition to the constitution; if

---

17. *Marbury v. Madison*, 1 Cr. (5 U.S.) 137 (1803).

both the law and the constitution apply to a particular case, so that the court must either decide that case conformable to law, disregarding the constitution; or conformable to the constitution disregarding the law; the court must determine which of these conflicting rules governs the case: this is of the very essence of judicial duty.

The existence of judicial review as a legitimate constitutional power was a reasonable inference from the status of the judiciary as an equal and coordinate branch of government under the separation of powers. A key question concerned the scope and effect of the power. In *Marbury v. Madison*, judicial review was limited in scope, referring to a statute dealing with the exercise of judicial duties. The logic of review, however, could be applied to legislative and executive acts in general. In the context of constitutional politics, it provided an incentive for government actors in policy controversies to submit constitutionally related questions to the judiciary for determination.

In view of this possibility, it is important to note a significant limitation on the judicial review function recognized by the Supreme Court in *Marbury v. Madison*.

Although the separation of powers justifies the judicial independence needed for judicial review, it also points to an alternative approach to determining the meaning of the Constitution. This is the idea of departmental constitutional review as expressed in the doctrine of political questions. The logic of the separation principle suggests that each of the three branches of government has authority to determine constitutional meaning concerning subjects assigned to it by the Constitution. The underlying idea is that the duties of lawmakers, executive officers, and judges involve distinct powers requiring different kinds of competency and judgment. The basic distinction is between the legislative and executive departments on the one hand and the judicial department on the other. This is the distinction between law and politics that is a fundamental premise of the rule of law.

In *Marbury v. Madison,* Chief Justice Marshall enunciated the political questions doctrine based on the law-vs.-politics distinction. Marshall said the Constitution vested in the President "certain important political powers, in the exercise of which he is to use his own discretion, and is accountable to the country in his political character, and to his own conscience." Where the heads of departments act as political agents in cases in which the executive possesses a constitutional or legal discretion, "nothing can be more perfectly clear than that their acts are only politically examinable." By analogy, legislative acts, equally if not more discretionary in character, warranted the same consideration.

In contradistinction to political questions were questions of a judicial nature. Marshall noted that where a specific duty was assigned by law and individual rights depended on the performance of that duty, "the individual who considers himself injured, has a right to resort to the laws of his country for a remedy." In other words, where the issue at stake was of a judicial nature, determination through the exercise of judicial authority was constitutionally proper.

The idea of the Constitution as fundamental law presumed the distinction between law and politics as modes of authority and competence. The distinction was necessary to prevent the rule of law from collapsing into the rule of men, which is to say rule by accident, force, expediency, and arbitrary will.

Politics proceeded through reflection, deliberation, and discretionary judgment about right political action for the common good. The rule of law proceeded on the basis of legal determinations arrived at through impartial application of principles, rules, and standards for the administration of justice. Although the spheres of law and politics needed to be distinguished in order that the purposes of each might be fulfilled, they could not be completely separated. In the practical resolution of constitutional controversies, therefore, it was often difficult to distinguish between the relative influence of law and politics in governmental action.

From the beginning of the government, federal and state courts were involved in political controversy to a limited extent. With respect to economic liberty and property rights, for example, judicial decisions concerning the Contract Clause of the Constitution affected public policy. As a general matter, however, judicial review was accepted as constitutionally legitimate in principle while being narrowly defined and sparingly exercised in practice. This changed in the late 19th century. Responding to political, social, and intellectual influences in society, the federal judiciary involved itself more frequently in public policy controversies arising from industrial economic development.

Fearing social upheaval, courts adopted a broad conception of liberty and property rights requiring protection against state economic regulation and working-class violence. The ideas guiding free-market legal protection, known as *laissez faire* jurisprudence, included security of liberty and property rights for individuals, entrepreneurial liberty, opposition to class legislation favoring particular groups in society, and recognition of business corporations as legal persons.

The most controversial legal principle was the judicial interpretation of the Due Process Clause of the Fourteenth Amendment as a substantive limitation on the exercise of state regulatory power. The doctrine of substantive due process was distinguished from the traditional form of procedural due process used in the administration of criminal law. Economic due process functioned as a ban on legislation that interfered unreasonably or unjustly with private property rights and economic freedom. It was the key interpretive innovation that signified a new kind of judicial review.

Modern judicial review differed from Founding-era judicial review in its understanding of the standard by which a court should determine whether a legislative act conformed or failed to conform to the Constitution. In early judicial review, the duty of the court was to determine whether an exercise of legislative power, when called into question in a particular case, existed as a constitutional power either by express reference to the text of the Constitution or by inference from the text. If the power was in the Constitution, then the manner, extent, or purpose of its exercise was a question of political judgment beyond the competence of the judiciary. If a legislative act was believed wrong in its purpose and effect, the proper remedy lay in recourse to the electoral accountability of lawmakers to the people.

In modern judicial review, by contrast, courts determined the constitutionality of a legislative act by considering its reasonableness from the standpoint of the judiciary rather than from the standpoint of the political branch of government. The question was not whether the power exercised was within the scope of legislative authority conferred by the Constitution, but whether the motive, purpose, and effect of its exercise met a constitutional standard of reasonableness as determined by the judiciary.

In 1887, the Supreme Court explained the rationale of new judicial review in observing: "The courts are not bound by mere forms. They are at liberty—indeed they are under a solemn duty—to look at the substance of things, whenever they enter upon the inquiry whether the legislature has transcended the limits of its authority."[18] This shift in perspective in the exercise of judicial review provoked widespread criticism of "judicial legislation" and "government by judiciary" in the early 20th century.

The practice of new judicial review did not categorically supersede the older approach to judicial decision making. Most state laws that were challenged as unreasonable under the Due Process Clause of the Fourteenth Amendment were sustained in the courts. Moreover the reasonableness test in new judicial review retained elements traditionally used in making a determination of constitutionality. If a statute was clearly within the scope of the legislative power and bore a reasonable relationship to a legitimate legislative purpose, the constitutional standard was met. The emergence of new judicial review did not necessarily reduce judicial decision making to the level of personal, subjective, or ideological opinion.

Nevertheless, the shift in perspective broadened the range of judicial discretion. On the one hand, courts could follow the traditional model of judicial restraint, which treated legislation as presumably constitutional on the theory that responsible lawmakers exercised properly delegated or reserved powers to reach constitutionally legitimate ends. On the other hand, courts could deny the presumption of constitutionality and require a state to prove the constitutionality of a statute by meeting the requirement of reasonableness as defined by the judicial understanding of reasonableness. There was much truth in the observation of constitutional scholar Charles Grove Haines in 1908 that the courts were "continually called upon to deal with questions that are purely political and governmental; to enter, partially at least, into the realm of

---

[18.] *Mugler v. Kansas*, 123 U.S. 623, 661 (1887).

legislation; and to discuss questions of political, economic, and social theory."[19]

The nature of judicial review and the role of the judiciary in American government implicated in a significant way the issue of constitutional preservation through development of Founding-era principles of fundamental law. Progressive reformers opposed new judicial review as a usurpation of the popular will and legislative authority not provided for in the Constitution. Conservative supporters defended it as jurisprudentially sound and faithful to the intent of the Founders to limit legislative power for the sake of republican freedom and individual rights and liberties.

Throughout the period 1900 to 1930, debate over the constitutional propriety of judicial review simmered. Meanwhile the question of constitutional maintenance and preservation was posed in a second major political development that implicated the separation of powers principle: the creation of administrative regulatory institutions in the national government.

The separation of powers was a distinctly American constitutional principle designed to secure republican freedom by organizing government sovereignty in equal and coordinate branches. From the beginning of the government in 1789, controversy over the separation of powers involved rival claims by Congress and the President to the exercise of particular powers. After the Civil War, the separation of powers principle fell into disfavor as an outdated relic of 18th century political thought. Political reformers viewed it as an obstacle to the creation of modern administrative institutions that were needed to rise above the wasteful, corrupt, and inefficient congres-

---

[19.] Charles Grove Haines, *The Conflict over Judicial Powers in the United States to 1870* (New York: Columbia University Press, 1909), p. 117.

sional politics of the Gilded Age. The operational effect of the separation of powers was considered inimical to the spirit of nationalism and the demand for unity and power in government that were believed necessary to deal with the problems of modern economy and society.

The standard reform complaint was that Congress exercised too much power over national government administration at the expense of the presidency. Expansion of executive power alone was not the answer, however, since Presidents were as partisan and politically shortsighted as lawmakers.

The solution proposed by Progressive reformers from the 1880s to the 1930s was the creation of independent administrative agencies with authority to regulate large business corporations that threatened republican freedom and opportunity. Regulatory agencies would combine elements of legislative, executive, and judicial authority in what can be thought of as a fourth branch of government: a non-political administrative branch. Created by Congress and appointed by the President, the agencies would exercise regulatory power in defined spheres of policy according to scientific principles of public administration.

In a narrow sense, the constitutional question was whether Congress could delegate legislative power to administrative officers in the executive branch or in independent regulatory agencies. In a series of late 19th century decisions dealing with minor policy issues, the Supreme Court held that Congress could confer on agencies administrative discretion to make rules having the force of law without violating the constitutional principle of the separation of powers, which prohibited the delegation of legislative power. In a broad sense, the question was whether the popular demand for national economic regulation as represented in the Progressive reform movement required a fundamental revision of the separation of powers as an obstacle to national unity and power.

By 1930, the creation of a wide variety of regulatory agencies, from the Interstate Commerce Commission of 1887 to the Federal Trade Commission of 1914 to the Radio Commission Act of 1927, was evidence that something like a national administrative state had come into existence. The question then arose whether the development of an administrative state was consistent with the constitutional principles of the Founding.

The Great Depression of the 1930s precipitated a political crisis comparable in significance to that of the Civil War era. Long-developing social and economic changes led to policy controversies that called into question the meaning of basic constitutional principles. Economic conditions threatened the sense of social welfare and security on which national stability and prosperity depended. In circumstances that seemed to demand unified government action to overcome economic and social dislocation, the principles of federalism and the separation of powers doctrine were deemed hopelessly inefficient and obstructionist. Reformers further viewed traditional legal protection of liberty and property rights of individuals and corporations in the free market as intellectually obsolete and morally irresponsible.

To restore national prosperity and social security, the New Deal Administration of Democrat President Franklin D. Roosevelt proposed a regulatory and reform program based on a reconceptualization of Founding-era constitutional principles. The natural rights of liberty, property, equality, and consent shifted from a personal individualist basis to a class and group rights basis. To a substantial extent, this theoretical move dissolved natural rights as the interest of individual citizens was considered subordinate to the public interest.

As a theoretical framework for the new liberalism, the notion of a "living Constitution" consisting in public opinion, political institutions, and governmental and legal practices was introduced as an alternative to or replacement of the Founders' Constitution. The written fundamental law could not literally be expunged, but its character could be changed by absorption into a living system of governmental institutions. To secure these new constitutional views, conservative guardianship of the written Constitution, sustained since the 1890s by *laissez faire*–minded, activist judicial review, would be superseded by the rule of liberal judges, content to practice judicial restraint and leave policymaking to the political branches of government.

Implemented in the course of President Roosevelt's unprecedented four consecutive Administrations, New Deal policies had far-reaching constitutional significance. In the political climate of the day, it was common for supporters and opponents alike to view the New Deal has a constitutional revolution intended either to update or uproot the old order of private property rights and limited government. Before considering its programmatic content, it is important to note a basic difference between the New Deal as a constitutional reform and earlier reform movements in the Reconstruction period and the Progressive era.

The New Deal differed by circumventing or failing to utilize the Article V amendment procedure, established by the Founders to correct errors and determine new constitutional meaning. Instead, the Roosevelt Administration chose to establish new interpretations of the Constitution through the revision of constitutional law. This meant electoral approval and legislative enactment of a reform agenda, enforcement by executive and administrative agency rule-making, and confirmation of the constitutionality of New Deal measures through the exercise of judicial review in the Supreme Court. Justifiable as this approach may have been on pragmatic political grounds, it reflected the new liberalism's radical challenge to orthodox constitutionalism.

The principal constitutional objective of New Deal liberalism was to expand the authority and responsibility of the federal government in the operation of the national economy. This included regulation of industrial and agricultural production, interstate commerce, money and banking, labor relations, unemployment, social welfare and security, housing, flood control, and conservation of natural resources. Policy centralization on this order of magnitude required repudiation of the conservative, localist, "states' rights" interpretation of the federal principle. A new kind of cooperative system of intergovernmental relations was legislated and administratively enforced, based on instruments such as federal grants-in-aid to states acting as agents of the national government.

Expansion of executive power over policymaking and administration was a logical means of nationalizing economic regulation. From the standpoint of Franklin D. Roosevelt, it could also be viewed as a constitutional end in itself. The Founders created a powerful office of chief executive under the separation of powers principle. Throughout the 19th century, Congress and the President vied for control of government administration, with Congress holding the upper hand most of the time. The ambition of Presidents Theodore Roosevelt and Woodrow Wilson to augment executive authority was part of the Progressive legacy inherited by Franklin D. Roosevelt.

This legacy was given a significant measure of realization in the Executive Reorganization Act of 1939, a landmark statute that established the contours of the modern presidency. The act created the Executive Office of the President, elevated the White House staff to the status of institutional entity, transferred the Bureau of the Budget to executive supervision, and gave the President authority to reorganize administrative agencies. Long demanded by previous chief executives, the rationale of executive reorganization was to give the President policy and administrative authority commensurate with his political responsibility as national leader in Progressive constitutional theory.

If history does not conform to Progressive ideology as reformers would like, it is at least cumulative in the sense that the changes of one era are taken up or absorbed in another where they present themselves in a different aspect. The political character of the New Deal as a liberal, reformist, radical, or revolutionary development was controversial to contemporaries.

Seventy-five years after the New Deal, important features of regulatory state liberalism maintain prominent institutional existence and significant public support. In many respects, constitutional and public policy controversies in the 21st century reflect those of the New Deal era, including the nature and scope of executive power, federal–state relations, government regulation of society and the economy, and the rights and liberties of individuals and social groups. While new moral and cultural issues such as abortion, environmentalism, and homosexual rights have emerged to roil contemporary politics, controversy persists about the meaning of basic constitutional principles. The jury is still out, therefore, concerning the constitutional significance of regulatory welfare state liberalism.

It is relevant to ask whether New Deal government, law, and policy built on and preserved or rejected and abandoned the Founders' Constitution. From both a historical and a normative point of view, the question admits of no easy answer. Federalism, the separation of powers, republican freedom and consent, and the Constitution as fundamental law and judicial review continue to define the parameters of constitutional politics. This fact can be taken as an indication of historical stability and continuity.

From a normative standpoint, however, 20th century constitutional change presents itself in a different light. The principles of the Founding embodied in the Constitution are directed to the end of limited government under the rule of law for the sake of responsible individual liberty, social freedom, and national independence. Of these principles, the substantive meaning of republican freedom in particular, considered in the light of the Founders' purpose and intent, best affords insight into the political and moral character of American constitutionalism in the 21st century.

Chapter 5

CONVOLUTIONS OF REPUBLICAN FREEDOM IN THE 21ST CENTURY

*F*rom the Founding era through the 19th century, republican freedom meant the individual natural right of personal liberty and the exercise of civil rights and liberties, including the right to own property, make contracts, enjoy the equal protection of the laws and legal process, speak, write, assemble, and worship freely. Political freedom and popular self-government under a system of constitutional government provided the background conditions necessary for the exercise of individual civil rights. The principal threat to liberty was believed to come from the exercise of arbitrary and unlimited power by rulers for their own privilege and benefit.

Constitutional republican liberty was therefore described as "liberty against government." This term correctly referred to the absence of restraint in virtue of which free persons exercised their faculties for their own interests and happiness.

In the 20th century, natural rights republican liberty was misleadingly characterized as "negative liberty." Progressive critics led the way, declaring *laissez faire* individual rights liberty to be a false freedom. In the Progressive view, persons deprived of material goods and resources, whether through the accidents of birth, social status, or the distribution of wealth under market competition, were incapable of exercising civil rights. To experience true liberty, it was necessary to revise bad social and economic arrangements and make new ones providing for the redistribution of wealth to the end of social justice. In the new liberal system of so-called positive liberty, republican freedom would depend on government intervention in the social and economic order. Public law and policy should confer rights of provision by which individuals belonging to specified groups and classes would acquire the capacity to exercise their rights. Instead of being threatened by the exercise of government power, as in *laissez faire* individualism, true liberty required positive acts of government regulation to redress unjust social conditions.

In 1932, presidential candidate Franklin D. Roosevelt proposed "an economic declaration of rights" and "an economic constitutional order." After the failure of his plan to pack the Supreme Court in 1937, Roosevelt appointed new justices willing to repudiate *laissez faire* legal principles. The Court began a long-range experiment in constitutional interpretation intended to modernize the equal rights core of the Founders' concept of republican freedom. The central aim was to transform the content of republican liberty from its historic focus on the individual rights of persons to a concern for the public-interest rights of persons in their identity as members of designated groups and classes. In promoting this project, liberal judges claimed the authority of modern judicial review to make public policy as a counterweight to, if not in defiance of, legislative policymaking under the principle of the separation of powers.

The modern liberal redefinition of republican freedom insisted on the distinction between property rights and economic liberty on the one hand and civil rights and civil liberties on the other. Implicit in this distinction was the legal and moral privileging of civil liberty over economic liberty.

According to the rationale offered by the Supreme Court in *U.S. v. Carolene Products Co.* (1938),[20] a double standard of judicial review was needed to compensate for the imperfection and inadequacy of representative democracy. Legislation that on its face appeared to be within a specific prohibition of the Bill of Rights as incorporated in the Fourteenth Amendment warranted stricter judicial scrutiny than legislation that regulated social and economic activity. With respect to the latter, the traditional presumption of constitutionality normally accorded state action was narrower in its operation. The Court further suggested that legislation restricting democratic processes that ordinarily could be expected to bring about the repeal of undesirable measures and legislation that curtailed the ability of particular religious, national, or racial minorities to utilize democratic processes to protect their rights and interests should be "subjected to more exacting scrutiny under the general prohibitions of the Fourteenth Amendment than are most other types of legislation."

The basic proposition underlying "strict scrutiny" judicial review was that democratic majorities could not be trusted to protect the rights of "discrete and insular minorities." During World War II and the Cold War, a time when national unity was highly valued, the double-standard conception of citizenship went through a slow gestation process. In the 1960s, the ascendancy of regulatory welfare state ideology provided the political support needed to put double-standard judicial review into practice.

---

20. *U.S. v. Carolene Products Co.*, 304 U.S. 144 (1938).

In the area of race relations, a good argument could be made that the individual rights standard of citizenship was inadequate and that something different and more effective was required. The system of state-mandated racial segregation and discrimination against black Americans, constitutionally affirmed by the Supreme Court in *Plessy v. Ferguson* (1896),[21] was the kind of egregious, majority-based denial of civil rights envisioned by proponents of double-standard judicial review. Nevertheless, when the Supreme Court declared in *Brown v. Board of Education* (1954)[22] that racially segregated public schools violate the Fourteenth Amendment, it relied on the nondiscrimination principle of racially impartial equal rights for individuals. Congress, too, in the Civil Rights Act of 1964 relied on the color-blind equal rights principle to prohibit unequal treatment and other forms of intentional discrimination in private employment on account of race, color, national origin, religion, or sex.

In the 1960s, however, social and political conditions were propitious for the application of double-standard judicial review. Spurred by the civil rights movement and the outbreak of racial violence, liberal lawyers, judges, and lawmakers were persuaded that judicial decision making, historically used to protect economic liberty and property rights, could be directed toward egalitarian reform purposes. Liberal judicial activism permitted the judiciary, ostensibly the branch of government least accountable to the will of the people, to promote social reform in the name of democracy. It authorized courts to act in a representative capacity, conferring on religious, racial, and ethnic minority groups a wide range of rights and benefits denied them by prejudicial legislative majorities.

[21.] *Plessy v. Ferguson*, 163 U.S. 537 (1896).
[22.] *Brown v. Board of Education*, 347 U.S. 483 (1954).

The result was that, in decisions concerning civil rights and liberties, legislative apportionment, criminal procedure, Social Security and welfare benefits, libel law, obscenity, and the right of privacy, the Supreme Court under Chief Justice Earl Warren developed the doctrine of substantive equal protection of the laws. Although the pace of liberal activist transformation of republican freedom has slowed since the 1970s, the general contours of this modern liberal jurisprudence remain in place.

A pervasive and aggressive attitude of rights consciousness inspired by liberal jurisprudence is one of the most prominent features of contemporary constitutional politics. Its intellectual premises are uncongenial to the natural law assumptions of the Founding era. In the view of the Founders, the basic rights of liberty, equality, consent, and property were harmonized in the natural law with duty, responsibility, and virtue in community and society. The basic rights of individuals entailed secondary rights that, depending on circumstances, were subject to regulation by republican political authority in the public interest.

By contrast, in contemporary legal thought, rights arise from subjective personal choice and will, epitomized in the concept of the "autonomous self." Rights are assumed to be superior to political authority, possessing qualities of absoluteness that immunize the rights claimant against public or private constraint. The right of privacy that has been imagined out of the Fourteenth Amendment illustrates this phenomenon. The idea that objective standards of moral right exist external to the mind and will of individuals—a philosophical premise taken for granted in the Founding era—is dismissed in contemporary rights culture. Numerous groups across the political spectrum claim the protection of rights for needs or interests that they consider important. The modern liberal attitude widely shared by citizens, scholars, opinion leaders, and politicians is summarized in legal philosopher Ronald Dworkin's assertion that "rights are trumps."[23]

The expansion of positive welfare state liberalism since the 1960s to include moral and cultural issues such as abortion and homosexual rights in addition to its traditional socioeconomic concerns has not gone unchallenged. The rise of modern conservatism inspired criticism of the judicial activist creation—out of ideological whole cloth—of rights that bear no clear relationship to the text of the Constitution. Perhaps the most controversial example of this process was the development of the right of privacy in a line of decisions from *Griswold v. Connecticut* (1965)[24] to *Roe v. Wade* (1973)[25] to *Casey v. Planned Parenthood of Southeastern Pennsylvania* (1992)[26] to *Lawrence v. Texas* (2003).[27]

At one level, the issue was the legal definition of the right of privacy and its derivation from a thicket of constitutional provisions in the First, Fourth, Fifth, Ninth, and Fourteenth Amendments. At a deeper level, the question was the political and moral content of republican citizenship and the nature and competence of judicial authority in the design of the Constitution. Judicial creation of rights implied that the meaning of republican freedom was a matter of legal interpretation to be decided by the Supreme Court rather than a political question concerning the basic principles of American nationality

23. Ronald Dworkin, *Taking Rights Seriously* (Cambridge, Mass.: Harvard University Press, 1977), p. xi.
24. *Griswold v. Connecticut*, 381 U.S. 479 (1965).
25. *Roe v. Wade*, 410 U.S. 113 (1973).
26. *Casey v. Planned Parenthood of Southeastern Pennsylvania*, 505 U.S. 833 (1992).
27. *Lawrence v. Texas*, 539 U.S. 558 (2003).

to be decided by the people as constituent power through representative institutions established by the Constitution.

If the courts could create rights, where did they derive the authority to do so? The conventional liberal argument, citing Article III defining the judicial power in conjunction with the Supremacy Clause in Article VI declaring the Constitution the supreme law of the land, was no longer sufficient justification. Criticism of judicial liberalism from the standpoint of the intent of the Framers, advanced by conservative scholars starting in the 1960s, brought the debate over the role of judicial review in American government—and the very nature of the Constitution itself—into the political arena. Defenders of judicial activist rights-creation and policymaking were forced to go outside the Constitution and appeal to the notion of an unwritten, evolving, "living Constitution" based on present-day realities to justify their practices.

In 1985, responding to the theory of original intent jurisprudence presented by Attorney General Edwin Meese, Justice William J. Brennan summarized the case for modern judicial liberalism. Brennan's basic proposition was that the Constitution "embodies the aspiration to social justice, brotherhood, and human dignity that brought this nation into being." Conceding the relevance of the constitutional text, Brennan said that its genius lay in the adaptability of its principles to cope with current problems and needs. According to Brennan, constitutional interpretation reduced itself to the substantive value choices that each generation made to maintain, alter, or overrule the principles of the Founders. In this view, fidelity to the Constitution meant fidelity to the ever-changing content of the Framers' principles and aspirations, not to their intentions.

Justice Brennan defined judicial review as "the authority to give meaning to the Constitution." Denying that the intent of the Framers could be accurately understood outside of their specific historical context, he said the key to constitutional interpretation was to discover what the words and principles of the Constitution mean in contemporary society. Constitutional amendment under Article V was impractical. The alternative was for the Supreme Court to seek "the community's interpretation of the Constitutional text" through judicial determination of fundamental values on behalf of the people. The only permanent thing in the Constitution was the aspiration to justice and human dignity. Justice Brennan thus dissolved the text of the fundamental law into a warrant for judicial policymaking and constitutional invention.[28]

A standard theme in 20th century legal scholarship was the inevitably political character of judicial decision making, deriving from the opinions and values of judges and the nature of the law as an instrument of social control. From the New Deal to the 1960s, the ascendancy of liberalism in national politics insulated judicial activist constitutional interpretation against the charge of political judging. In the 1980s and 1990s, the emergence of original intent jurisprudence as a critique of legal liberalism to some extent leveled the playing field of constitutional politics.

At the same time, the division in public opinion between the two major parties, clearly identified as liberal Democrat and conservative Republican, resulted in significant periods of divided government in which each party controlled either Congress or the presidency. Ideological polarization transformed the judicial nomination process into an out-and-out political struggle. The bitterly contested nominations of Judge Robert Bork (1987) and Judge Clarence Thomas (1991) to the Supreme Court suggested that the judicial branch, under

---

[28.] Justice William J. Brennan, Jr., "To the Text and Teaching Symposium," Georgetown University, October 12, 1985.

pressure from the political branches as much as from the ideo-logical proclivity of judges, was becoming dangerously political.

From the outset, the performance of judicial duties had a political aspect that was the necessary consequence of the con-stitutional requirement of executive nomination to, and Senate confirmation of nominees to, the federal bench. To confer on political officers the power to determine who should be appointed to judicial office opened the possibility of political subversion of the rule of law. Common sense suggested, how-ever, that obvious politicization of the judicial function would defeat the purpose of having an independent judiciary to decide questions of a judicial nature involving individual lib-erty and property rights. The separation of powers was the institutional arrangement through which was expressed the distinction between the special competency of the legislative and executive branches on the one hand, and of the judicial branch on the other, that the Founders believed was essential to republican constitutional government.

The competency and qualification of elected lawmakers lay in their representative relationship to the needs, interests, values, and aspirations of the people as the constituent author-ity of the nation. The competency and qualification of judges with respect to the administration of justice lay in their mas-tery of legal principles, rules, and precedents, which together constrained subjective personal preference and encouraged the requisite judicial temperament. The practical reason intrinsic to the separation of powers directed the concern of the politi-cal branches toward particular and concrete decisions aimed at making good, wise, and just policy within the scope of consti-tutionally delegated powers. This reflected the decision of the people in the framing and ratification of the Constitution that political authority should be exercised by representative law-makers and executive officers. Analogously, the separation of powers directed the concern of the judicial branch to the application of legal principles and rules for the resolution of civil conflicts between individuals and between the community and persons accused of alleged criminal acts.

In recent years, politics in the United States has been conducted with a degree of ideological hostility that calls into question the stability of the constitutional order. Political opponents accuse each other of destroying the Constitution while seeking ways to criminalize their acts and opinions. In part, this robustness may reflect the tendency toward rhetorical excess that is characteristic of media-driven mass democracy. It is fair to ask, however, whether divided-government battles between Congress and the President that deepen the politicization of the judiciary are good for the Constitution or detrimental to it. It is possible for ceremonial veneration of the Constitution to continue at the same time that moral and operational fidelity to the fundamental law declines.

Unwarranted exercise of political power by the judiciary is perhaps the institutional disorder that has most threatened republican constitutionalism in the past half-century. The American political tradition places a premium, at least in a rhetorical sense, on "taking the Constitution seriously." What this actually means is, of course, debatable. At a minimum, however, it can be understood as resting on the common-sense assumption that the Framers said what they meant and meant what they said. The text of the Constitution, in other words, has an intrinsic and real meaning. The reason for having a written constitution was to create energetic government power and to limit the exercise of that power in a new way that would be consistent with the character of republican society. Conformity to the constitutional text, written in the clear and common language of the people, was the test of legitimate public policy.

There was room for debate in 19th century constitutional politics as to whether the requirement of "taking the Constitution seriously" was met in particular cases. In the theory of the "living Constitution" posited by 20th century Progressive reformers, however, the criterion of constitutional seriousness and fidelity was redefined in terms of political pragmatism.

In one sense, pragmatic constitutional fidelity was defined with reference to existing political and governmental arrangements and the ways in which public policy was made, irrespective of the forms and procedures stipulated in the written Constitution. In another sense, pragmatic constitutional "seriousness" referred to the intellectual and institutional transformation according to which the determination of constitutional meaning became the exclusive concern of the judiciary. Progressive critics of *laissez faire* jurisprudence in the late 19th and early 20th centuries objected to the growth of conservative judicial activism at the expense of popular majority-rule constitutionalism. In the period after 1945, liberal judicial activists, changing their tune, expanded both the scope of judicial constitutional interpretation and the policymaking power that it conferred on courts to the point where the charges of "judicial supremacy" and "government by judiciary" accurately described the state of constitutional politics.

The conservative critique of liberal judicial activism is premised on the idea that the Constitution should be understood and applied according to the original intent of those who wrote and ratified it. This principle is intrinsic to the project of written constitutionalism and formed the basis for the earliest legal commentaries stating rules of interpretation to be used in applying the Constitution. Throughout the 19th century, the logic of recognizing Framer intent as the first step in constitutional interpretation was taken for granted. Only toward the end of the 20th century, as a rebuke to judicial activist policymaking based on moral and philosophic sources external to the Constitution, was the idea of original intent jurisprudence systematically developed into a doctrine of evolving constitutional law.

CONCLUSION

*I*n assessing the present state of American constitutionalism, partisan warnings of impending disaster, of which there are many, should not be taken at face value. In a diverse and pluralistic society, disagreement over the meaning of the Constitution in relation to public policy is to be expected. It was for this reason that the Founders, in their concern for ordered liberty, established the Constitution on the principles of distributed, balanced, and limited power that have been examined in this essay.

From the beginning of the government, there was controversy over the meaning of basic constitutional principles, at times rising to the level of violence and armed conflict, and some might argue that partisan and ideological forces have so distorted the understanding of basic principles as to deprive them of any essential meaning. If this were the case, however, the words of the Constitution would be reduced to sheer indeterminacy, and constitutional debate would now be nothing more than an elaborate public fiction. The gravity and portent surrounding recent controversy over issues such as the appointment of federal judges and the scope of executive power suggest otherwise.

The words of the Constitution continue to have relevance and real meaning in American government and politics. This fact results from and is evidence of the practical reason built into the design of the Constitution as the charter of American nationality. National unity, freedom, and limited government are the basic values underlying and intrinsic to the principles of federalism, the separation of powers, republican liberty, and the Constitution as fundamental law. Because these principles together constitute a coherent whole, failure or derangement in one part may lead to disorder in the system as a whole.

The struggle for power between Congress and Presidents or disputes over the relative powers of the national and state governments may appear historically as the most obvious threat to constitutional order. There is an institutional familiarity in these disputes, however, which suggests that the participants can take care of themselves. The capacity of the legislative and executive branches, and of the federal and state governments, legitimately to represent the authority of the people creates a reasonably level playing field for constitutional politics. The authority of the judicial branch is different. Despite its seeming monopoly of constitutional interpretation, the judiciary is more vulnerable to constitutional attrition.

The Founders understood that politics and law are distinctive yet complementary modes of authority that are necessary to the establishment of collective social order. As the fundamental law of American government, the Constitution, with its institutional design based on the separation of powers, comprehends both types of authority. The system of checks and balances is a necessary adjunct of the separation of powers principle that preserves constitutional equilibrium by giving each branch a partial involvement in the exercise of power by the other branches. To a certain extent, this institutional arrangement mixes or complicates political and legal elements of constitutional authority, raising a series of questions about the proper relationship between the equal and coordinate branches of government.

Beyond its equilibrium function, the separation of powers served the end of republican government by recognizing the constituent sovereignty of the people in the representative character of the legislative and executive branches. By giving the judiciary the status of an equal and coordinate branch of government, the design of the Constitution implicitly recognized the need to reconcile popular republican government with the reason, justice, and impartiality of the rule of law.

That courts might interject themselves into political government was not seen as a serious threat. As Alexander Hamilton observed in *Federalist* No. 78, under the separation of powers system, "the judiciary, from the nature of its functions, will always be the least dangerous to the political rights of the constitution."[29] The more difficult challenge lay in making the Constitution effective in the conduct of government. This required that the political branches recognize limitations on the exercise of power that were written into the text of the fundamental law and implicit in the design of the separation of powers and the federal–state division of sovereignty.

Historically, centralization of power in the national government at the expense of the states and consolidation of power in the executive branch at the expense of the legislature have been perceived as the greatest threats to the survival of the Constitution. More recently, the power of the judiciary has been viewed as a threat to the political rights of the people.

Without denying the plausibility of these concerns, it is important to note a distinction. The accountability of political government to the people through the system of republican representation provides means by which the actions of law-

---

[29.] *Federalist* No. 78, p. 465.

makers and executives can be limited. No such restraint oper-
ates on the actions of judges. Moreover, many factors,
including support in the professional legal community and the
willingness of most lawmakers and executives to acquiesce in
judicial supremacy, encourage the extraordinary expansion of
judicial power that has occurred in the past half-century.

From the standpoint of activist judicial review, a case can
be made for the democratic character of government by judiciary. Defenders of judicial activism, while conceding its coun-
termajoritarian nature in a strict sense, argue that government
by judiciary is democratic because the Constitution itself is
democratic. In the words of one legal theorist, "constitutionalism *is* democracy—or at any rate it ought to be democracy, it
aspires to be democracy—over time."[30]

A more historically sound and constitutionally faithful
approach to the problem of government by judiciary centers
on the competence and qualifications of unelected judges in
the design of republican government. The Founders intended
to create an independent judiciary. Presidential nomination of
judges, with appointment contingent on the consent of the
Senate, is a check-and-balance mechanism that gives the political branches substantial influence over the composition of the
federal judiciary. The procedure does not rest on the presumption, however, that judges will be guided in the performance of
constitutional duty by their own partisan and ideological pref-
erences or those of legislative and executive officers.

On the contrary, the design of the Constitution recognizes
a substantive distinction between the spheres of politics and
law. In adopting the principle of the separation of powers, the
Founders expressed their considered judgment that questions

[30.] Jed Rubenfeld, *Revolution by Judiciary: The Structure of American Constitutional Law* (Cambridge, Mass.: Harvard University Press, 2005), p. 96.

of a legal nature arising under the Constitution were the proper concern of the judicial branch and that political questions were the proper concern of the legislative and executive branches.

It is obvious from the design of the Constitution, to say nothing of the Anglo–American legal tradition, that in the nature of the judicial process, judges lack the competence on which republican government depends. By virtue of professional training, experience, and disposition, judges lack the qualifications required for the prudential, discretionary, and politically informed deliberation demanded of lawmakers and executive officers in a republican constitution. Courts do not hold hearings, gather information, seek the opinion of constituents, and enact general and prospective statutes as rules of action in civil society. When judges presume to do so—on their own initiative, at the urging of legal theorists, or in consideration of the partisan and ideological interests of executives and lawmakers responsible for their appointment—they exceed the constitutional authority entrusted to them.

The paramount authority of the Constitution is not subject to revision by the judiciary any more than it is subject to revision by the political branches. To go back to fundamentals, the distinctive contribution of the judiciary to republican government consists in the duty not to regard as lawful, but as void, an act of legislative authority that, in the words of *Federalist* No. 78, is "contrary to the manifest tenor of the Constitution."[31] In Chief Justice John Marshall's concise summary, "the Constitution controls any legislative act repugnant to it."[32] The Founders' concept of limited republican government is incoherent if the Constitution is not recognized as

---

[31.] *Federalist* No. 78, p. 466.
[32.] *Marbury v. Madison*, at 137.

beyond the power of the political and judicial branches to alter. To assume otherwise is to substitute a subjective, metaphorical "living Constitution" for the objective, written Constitution of the Founding.

As in the Founding era, the nature of the Constitution is really the fundamental issue at stake. Knowledge and understanding of the Constitution should guide policymaking rather than the other way around. The Constitution is substantive in the sense that its framing and ratification signified in theory and actualized in practice the formation of the people of the United States as a nation and a self-governing political society. Of course, factors such as economy, language, religion, custom, and tradition, which in other countries form the ground of national identity, need to be taken into account. Considered together, they illuminate the historical context of American constitutionalism and give cultural inflection to a new kind of national identity based essentially on republican political ideals and institutions.

As they have throughout their history, Americans in the 21st century have reason to be concerned about the survival of the Constitution. As written fundamental law, the Constitution provides a framework and normative account of the ends, principles, and institutions of government suitable to the character of a republican people. Among modern political societies, Americans are distinctive in their attachment to the written Constitution as the measure of political and governmental legitimacy.

The fidelity that Americans profess rests on the conviction that the Constitution of the Founding establishes institutions of republican self-government that are indispensable to the preservation of individual and national freedom. And this popular fidelity to the Constitution is no less indispensable because, in George Washington's words, "the preservation of the sacred fire of liberty and the destiny of the republican model of government are justly considered, perhaps, as deeply, as finally, staked on the experiment entrusted to the hands of the American people."[33]

[33.] George Washington, "First Inaugural Address," April 30, 1789, in *The Writings of George Washington from the Original Manuscript Sources*, 1745–1799, ed. John C. Fitzpatrick (Washington: U.S. Government Printing Office, 1931–1944), Vol. 30, pp. 294–295.

ABOUT THE AUTHOR

*H*erman Belz, Ph.D., is a professor of history at the University of Maryland and academic director of the James Madison Memorial Fellowship Foundation in Washington, D.C. He is the author of several books, including *Abraham Lincoln, Constitutionalism, and Equal Rights in the Civil War Era* (1998); *A Living Constitution or Fundamental Law? American Constitutionalism in Historical Perspective* (1998); and *Equality Transformed: A Quarter Century of Affirmative Action* (1991). He is also co-author of *The American Constitution: Its Origin and Development* (7th ed., 1991).

In 2004, Dr. Belz was appointed to the National Council on the Humanities. He has received numerous awards, including fellowships from the John Simon Guggenheim Memorial Fellowship Foundation, the Earhart Foundation, and the Social Philosophy and Policy Center at Bowling Green State University. In 2001–2002, he was a visiting scholar in the James Madison Program in American Ideals and Institutions at Princeton University. Dr. Belz was educated at Princeton University and received his M.A. and Ph.D. degrees in history from the University of Washington.